THE BIGGEST SHORT GUY

"The amazing untold story of Walter Beran The CPA Who Changed LA"

FRANK A. PAUL AND JAMES P. BERAN

THE LONG AND SHORT OF IT – Laker "Magic"
Johnson and Chamber President Walter Beran kid each
other about their respective heights. Southern California
Business, Nov. 11, 1981

Table of Contents

Introduction

I n the nation's second largest city of Los Angeles, there are few prominent people—past or present—not well known to the general public. This book is about a major exception. While Walter Beran was an icon to the L.A. elite in his day, he was the sort of man who didn't worry about the credit or his own personal brand; at least, not in the way luminaries do today. He took the stage when asked and had a profound impact from there, but he enjoyed working behind the scenes and promoting the causes of the many influential people who called upon his acumen, support, and friendship—historic figures like long-time Mayor Tom Bradley, former President and First Lady Ronald and Nancy Reagan, former ARCO chief Lod Cook, former head of Toyota Motors U.S.A, Yuki Togo, and many others.

The Biggest Short Guy is the sort of story that is increasingly rare in today's hyper-connected world. News of anyone doing anything significantly good or bad travels fast and is devoured widely. Add to that the ease with which we can uncover a virtual history of anyone in minutes, and it's easy to see why being unheard of is quite unheard of. Yet an online search of Walter Beran would yield a notable yet paltry biography, largely from his *L.A. Times* obituary. However, the effect of his accomplishments are still widespread today. Walter Beran was a man who arguably shaped the soul of Los Angeles more than any contemporary from the 1970s-1990s. To accomplish this as a city official, philanthropist or entertainer would not be surprising. To accomplish this as an accountant is almost unbelievable.

Yet that was the primary channel through which he repaired and enlightened a community fractured along unjust racial, religious, and societal lines. It is not an understatement to say that Los Angeles and a great number of its residents would not be where they are today if a small, poor, orphaned boy from Texas named Walter had not called their city home for the last 35 years of his life. Their city's broken history began to heal as his history was written into it. In the end, their healing rewrote his story as well.

Dedication

This book is dedicated to my parents, who in some way still show me every day that love is the only thing in life that matters; to the millions of businessmen and women in America and around the world who give selflessly of their time, money and love to the communities in which they serve; to all those in the U.S. Armed Services, past, present and future...heroes all; and to Mrs. Nancy Reagan, the strongest person my father ever knew.

Acknowledgements

To my friends and family: you make life rock. All my love, always.

To my father's brothers — John, Ernest, Bennie and Rosy Symm — all since passed, who made the sacrifices and laid the foundation for my father to become the amazing man he became.

To Dr. David Feinberg, Dr. Jeffery Eckardt, Dr. Charles Forscher, Dr. Michael Selch, Kathy Dezeeuw and all the staff at Ronald Reagan UCLA and Cedars Sinai Hospitals without whose skill and dedication I would not have lived to see this book to its conclusion, and who have made every day forward possible.

To Rich Melcombe, Glenn Llopis and John Nackel, and Shelley Tang, who lit the path for this book to be written.

To Bennett Tramer, a great friend and mentor who helped give this book its soul.

To Dr. Keith Phillips, a real hero in a world of faux heroes.

To the Japan America Society, and the country and people of Japan, whose kindness has always been overwhelming and heartfelt.

To the City of Angels and its people.

To Mr. Jim Turley and all the fantastic people of the EY family.

Endorsements

"Walter Beran gave that which is most precious in life; his time. No challenge was too great, no task to small. He did not seek recognition or financial gain. His commitments and contributions to Los Angeles are still felt today."

Peter Ueberroth
Former Commissioner of Baseball & Past Chairman United States Olympic Committee

"Walter Beran set the standard for ethical business conduct in Los Angeles. His clarion call for businesses to give back to the community reflected his high moral standards. He was a servant-leader, who elevated all who knew him."

Dr. Keith Phillips
Founder, World Impact, Inc.

"Walter Beran was an influential civic leader who admirably served his nation as a decorated war hero, an envoy to Japan, and a trusted advisor to business leaders and government officials."

Michael D. Antonovich
Los Angeles County Supervisor

"Walter Beran was a giant among men. His stature was not measured in feet and inches, but rather in the greatness of his heart, the depth of his wisdom, and the kindness of his character. Integrity, humility, and generosity were the hallmarks of his life. We would all do well to model ourselves after him."

Buddy Owns, Teaching Pastor,
Saddleback Church, Lake Forest, CA

"Walter Beran's service as chairman of Japan America Society of Southern California not only set a mark of excellence all his successors strive to achieve, he lifted the Society and U.S.—Japan business relationships to a new level of engagement and commitment to the communities in which they serve. *The Biggest Short Guy* is a must read for anyone who wants to learn how to make a significant, long lasting and positive impact on his or her business, community and philanthropic endeavors."

Douglas G. Erber
President, Japan America Society of Southern California

Foreword

W hat does every person want from life? Oh sure...fame, fortune, family, good health, the bright lights of Hollywood, yada
yada yada.

Actually, what we really want is to touch the lives of others. To
leave an impact on the world we live in. To earn the respect and admiration of others. To have the love of our children. To be remembered
after we are gone.

This is a story about a remarkable man who achieved all of those
things. He was a business icon in one of the biggest and most bustling
cities in the world, who never forgot his roots in a 400-person Texas
town. A decorated war hero whose service to others didn't end at the
completion of World War II. A man who tirelessly travelled the world,
but never forgot that the love of his life was back at home. A man who
made extraordinary contributions to the firm where he spent his career,
but whose broader impact outside Ernst & Young exceeded his impact
inside it.

When Jim Beran told me he was writing a book about his father
Walter, I was delighted. When he asked me to write the Foreword, I was
both humbled and terrified. You see, Walter really was a legend in the
firm I had the honor to lead. He was the Vice Chairman of our firm's
Western Region at the time of his retirement in 1986, a role he held
for fifteen years. The next year, when as a new partner I moved to our
national office to lead a client relations department (which Walter had
led many years prior), all I heard was that nobody had ever seen anybody build and maintain relationships better than Walter. As important

as those relationships were for our firm, far more important was the legacy of giving back to one's community that Walter left with us. Long before it was recognized by business people the world over, Walter realized that (in his words), "If the community around them is not healthy, their businesses eventually will suffer." Boy, did he live those words; lending his time, talent and treasure to help the world in countless ways.

It is this legacy of investing in relationships and investing in the community that has carried forward within Ernst & Young to this day, and which guides the firm to do its part in Building a Better Working World.

Thank you, Walter, for your gifts to the firm. Thank you, Jim, for writing this gift of wisdom and inspiration to a world of readers.

James S. Turley
Chairman and Chief Executive Officer (2001-2013)
Ernst & Young

1

Hallways

Capistrano Beach, CA
June, 2007

A stocky 53-year-old merged his silver Lexus onto Pacific Coast Highway between San Diego and Los Angeles. After two quick turns, he accelerated up a steep incline to a stretch of sandstone bluffs that faced the ocean. A condominium complex was there and the driver pulled to a stop on the backside of one unit.

The driver's name was Jim and the condo was where his father planned to retire and enjoy the books and wine he'd been collecting since the 1950's. The breezy 400-square-foot balcony was idyllic for both; but the man never found the time before he died.

While he retired two decades prior to his death, Jim's father couldn't bear to leave his old neighborhood 70 miles to the north. The community there was rich and full of too many good memories. After he retired, he and Jim's mother stayed put and the condo became an upscale storehouse. Now the man was gone and his clothes needed to be removed.

Jim slid from his SUV and entered the condo through the garage, passing crates of wine and boxes marked with black Sharpie. As he stepped into the kitchen, his heart tightened at the scent. It was a stale and unpleasant scent, but it was familiar and it carried warm thoughts. Jim exhaled and headed toward the stairs.

Hanging on the wall opposite the stairwell was a large black and white photo of his parents, mouths wide and eyes smiling as they fed each other a messy hunk of wedding cake. The photo was a gift from him and his older brother for their parents' fiftieth wedding anniversary. Jim stared at it, letting his eyes scan the names of those who'd signed the photo and offered congratulations. They were familiar names and all were attached to stories his dad told him over the years.

Jim turned and headed up the stairs, looking over the photos climbing the wall—high school headshots of him and his older brother, and next to them were headshots of his dad and mom as young students. At the top, he turned down a hall that led to an office and back bedroom. Along both walls hung his father's proudest keepsakes. The two Purple Hearts and Bronze Star his father won in World War II were pinned neatly behind the same rectangle of glass. Jim grinned when he recalled his father's typical quip on how he won the Bronze Star: "I ran the wrong way."

Next to the medals hung a poem about an old French woman his dad met in St. Nazaire as an eighteen-year-old soldier; her words had lingered a lifetime. Beside the poem, and behind another rectangle of glass, was the dagger a German soldier surrendered on V-E Day. Across the hall were three framed clippings. The first was from a 1973 article on a local reunion of U.S.S. Leopoldville survivors. The second was an excerpt from a 1982 *Los Angeles Times* interview of his father, who was then president of the Los Angeles Area Chamber of Commerce. Jim's eyes picked a spot, and he read his father's words:

> *Many don't seem to realize that if the community around them is not healthy, their business eventually will suffer. Our compassion must become less institutional and more personal.*

The third clipping was an excerpt from a speech his father gave at the 1976 Town Hall of California. Jim laughed as he came across the story his father used to open the speech, which was on the topic of business ethics:

> *Two executives were having a drink at a club when one asked the other how his company selected its*

auditing firm. "Well," the one executive replied, "it was very easy. We called in the managing partners of three firms and we asked each of them the same question. The question was: 'How much is two plus two?' Two of them came up with four as the answer. But when the managing partner of the third firm was asked the same question, he replied, 'Well, gentlemen, what figure did you have in mind?'"

Jim turned through the doorway on the left and entered the office. His eyes scanned the wall of books neatly organized behind the desk: the complete works of Ibsen, Melville, and Shelley, alongside *The Life and Opinions of Tristram Shandy*, *How to Win Friends and Influence People*, and many novels and books of poetry, some in their original German language.

Small picture frames leaned against books on the lower levels. They featured photos spanning five decades: one was of his father next to longtime Los Angeles Mayor Tom Bradley; another of his father standing with a group of well-dressed black boys in front of the California Club; the next of his father and mother laughing with the Emperor and Empress of Japan; and another of his father standing at the 1984 Summer Olympics with Peter Ueberroth, sixth commissioner of baseball and former chairman of the United States Olympic Committee. Two dozen more photos peppered the walls and sat atop the office furniture alongside mementos. One of them was a framed document announcing that his father was the autumn 1986 recipient of the "Order of the Rising Sun, Gold Rays with Neck Ribbon," one of the highest honors given by the Japanese government to an American citizen. There were few awards of which his father was more proud, but the item next to it, resting alone in a clear box, was the gift no other surpassed: a bullet shell from the twenty-one-gun salute at Ronald Reagan's funeral.

On the wall opposite the books hung another clipping from the *Los Angeles Times*. It announced his father's retirement in the fall of 1986. The title read: "Retired but Hardly Retiring."

Jim breathed it all in again and then he slipped behind his father's desk. That's when his eyes met the photo that captured his father's essence as well as any. He lifted it in front of him. It was a candid shot of his parents, well-dressed and laughing alongside a half-dozen friends at a festive dinner table. Jim turned the picture over and read the date: 1985, the final year of their legendary Christmas party.

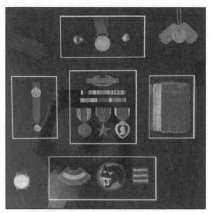

WWII Medals, Decorations and New
Testament Bible

Order of the Rising Sun

2

Head of the Line

Beverly Hills, CA
December 1, 1985

The receiving line for a black-tie Christmas party stretched down the hallway outside the grand ballroom doors of the famous Beverly Wilshire Hotel. Among those in line were Los Angeles Mayor Tom Bradley, U.S. Ambassador to Japan Jim Hodgson, beloved comedian Phyllis Diller, *L.A. Times* publisher Otis Chandler, ARCO CEO Lod Cook, President of Disney Michael Eisner, Los Angeles Dodgers owner Peter O'Malley, former Postmaster General Marvin Watson, and the World War II legend General Omar Bradley, the last living five-star field commander. Interspersed with them in smiling conversation were other local celebrities—actors, musicians, Los Angeles city officials, and corporate VIPs, including the CEOs of Bank of America, Union Bank, and Wells Fargo, the presidents of Toyota and Mitsubishi North America, and the chairman of the USC School of Business.

At the head of the line and facing the crowd stood a 5' 4", square-jawed businessman, four months from sixty and nine months from retirement. Next to him stood his petite, spirited wife Annette whom everyone called "Speedy." The "Who's Who" of Los Angeles stood in line, some for nearly an hour, to shake his hand and greet his bride.

Every great city had its builders—those key individuals who shaped the culture and its skyline through their work. Every great city also had its foreman—the one individual from whom the city's builders found their resources and inspiration. In Los Angeles, from the mid-1970s to the mid-1990s, that man was Walter Beran. He moved his family to the City of Angels in 1972 to become Partner in charge for for all the western states clients of the financial giant then known as Ernst & Ernst (eventually Ernst & Young). His friends knew this was only his day job.

Standing beside his bride of thirty-seven years, Walter greeted each guest with a lively, "Merry Christmas!" The greeting triggered a peculiar smile in each recipient. Walter was known to offer the salutation quite liberally, any time of year. Now for him to offer the greeting in December seemed almost odd–for once, it was actually fitting!

It would take an hour for all 500 guests to receive their personal welcome and find their assigned tables. The official celebration began promptly at 7:00 PM.

The grand ballroom was arranged with fifty tables classically adorned in crimson linens and white floral centerpieces with gold and silver accoutrements. A twelve-piece stringed orchestra filled the room with holiday classics from Crosby, Sinatra, Cole, and Garland. Were you to crash the Christmas party, you would quickly conclude that Walter had come from a blue-blooded pedigree. The handmade décor, the imported finery, even his and Speedy's attire—he in his black wool tuxedo and she in her navy satin gown beneath a thin silver shawl—sung resources and affluence; generations of it. Surely, one or both had been handed down some advantage.

Christmas Party with Mayor Tom Bradley

3

Salt of the Earth

Central Texas
April 1926

Walter grew up in The Grove, Texas, a tiny unincorporated community in the Hill Country, approximately thirty-five miles southwest of Waco and eighty miles northeast of Austin. Its name was bestowed in 1859 by a small community of cotton farmers who built their lives among a large grove of Texas live oaks flanking the edge of the Leon River Valley. A decade later, a group of German Lutheran immigrants settled alongside the farmers and gave The Grove a personality. While the town's economy was sustained by the cotton industry, its body and soul were fed by the Lutheran church, a knack for home-brewing, and a well that never ran dry. By the 1920s, The Grove reached its diminutive peak of four hundred residents—large enough to be counted, but small enough that Walter would later quip they shared their town drunk with the neighboring town.

Walter was the youngest of four sons born in The Grove to Frank and Thelma Beran, third generation descendants from the town's original German Lutheran settlers. If being the baby in a tribe of boys was not bad enough, Walter was also the runt of the litter. He would remain the smallest by several inches, even when the four brothers were full-grown. There was also the misfortune of sharing a birthday—April 20th—with an Austrian-born German named Adolf Hitler. The association would mean nothing in 1926, the year in which Walter was born and during which Hitler released his second volume of *Mein Kampf*. However, a season was coming when Walter would ponder the connection.

Like all residents of The Grove, the Berans spoke English and German and readily followed the mores of the Lutheran faith. This required church every Sunday, regular midweek gatherings, and a *zeitgeist* framed by the golden rule and grace, not in the least part because Lutherans, especially the Germanic variety, enjoyed their drink.

On the whole, The Grove was a quiet self-made community that enjoyed its anonymity. The town had no city square because its footprint was merely a straight, north-to-south line consisting of a dusty main street flanked by the Planters State Bank, a doctor's office, a post office, a police station, a blacksmith, the Cocklebur Saloon, and the town jewel known as the W. J. Dube General Store, selling everything from coffins to coffee. Just outside of town sat the schoolhouse, the cemetery, and the white steepled Lutheran church nestled between the large branches of a few live oaks.

To say the town was poor is a relative statement. It was simple. Residents of The Grove knew nothing more than what they had—farming, ranching, and good fellowship—and what they had was plenty enough. That is not to say there weren't families with more and others with less. The phrase "dirt poor" wasn't coined until the Great Depression was two years old, but it certainly could have described the Berans' lot.

Walter's family of six paid five dollars a month for a 500-square foot, four-room shanty on the west end of the main street. A thick crack ran diagonally across the middle of the floor, from front corner to back. It tugged apart the wooden planks enough in some spots that a small hand could reach through the crevice and scoop a handful of dirt. Outside, tall dry grass brushed against the wooden siding, and an oak off the small front porch offered occasional respites from the sun. Out back were fields upon fields of cotton owned by a local farmer that stretched a quarter mile toward the western horizon. Walter would come to know that arid soil well as a young boy, but before he learned the meaning of hard work, life forced on him a much harsher lesson.

It was a Saturday afternoon in the fall of 1927. Eighteen-month old Walter was napping in the bedroom when his father, Frank Beran, stepped through the front door of their home with a loaded shotgun hanging from his shoulder. He'd been hunting, but had no game to show for it. Standing inside talking were Walter's mother and her sister's husband. Without warning Frank swung the shotgun forward and opened fire, pumping three rounds at his wife and her brother-in-law. Then he dropped the gun and fled.

Twenty minutes later Benny, Walter's second oldest brother, approached the ramshackle house and heard Walter crying inside. Just then, Ernest, the second youngest brother, ran up behind him.

"Daddy's in the well!" he shrieked. "Daddy's in the well!"

Benny stopped short of entering the house. Instead, he turned and sprinted to the town well where he peered over the edge. Frank Beran was curled up at the bottom. Benny immediately circled back to their house and flung open the front door. Sprawled on the floor in pools of blood were his mother and uncle.

***

The owner of the town's general store, W. J. Dube, was a Beran-family friend who knew the governor in Austin. He placed a phone call to him and shortly thereafter, Frank Beran was removed from the well by authorities and placed in a holding cell where he spent the night. A car arrived the following morning and transported him to the Austin State Hospital (originally known as the Texas State Lunatic Asylum), a broad, three-story building with thick limestone walls and high ceilings meant to offer relief from the Texas heat. Frank joined some 1,000 patients residing there in shared rooms with one window to the outside. It would be the only home he would know from that day forward.

While Thelma Beran remained unconscious and in critical condition in the hospital, her brother-in-law died from his wounds. Yet there was no formal arrest, no charges filed, and no trial. The malefactor was simply made to disappear, along with the murder he committed.

No one ever uncovered why it happened, nor did anyone seek to. The details were a hornet's nest better left untouched. It was deduced that Frank Beran had a mental illness that lay dormant until one Saturday afternoon in 1927, when it awoke in a rage.

There would be no trace of the tragedy except in the scars and suppressed memories of The Grove's residents. The expunction was good for the Beran boys' futures. They would not be branded with the sins of their father. Still, it was only a consolation as it did not alter the reality that Walter and his three older brothers no longer had a father and their mother would be gone for a very long time.

***

No one knows the origin of the word "grove," but its primary meaning for more than 1,000 years has remained the same. It is a small grouping of trees that bind themselves together over time, both above ground and below it. The trees' branches become intertwined with one another, providing stability to the grove in severe storms. The trees' roots also grow together, strengthening the stature of every individual trunk.

Whether The Grove's first settlers considered the metaphor when they named the town is unknown, but even if the association was never pronounced by the residents; it was illustrated in their actions.

Once Frank and Thelma Beran were gone, the people of The Grove stepped in and raised the four brothers as their own. One resident took on a particularly maternal role. Her name was Rosie Symm, the Beran boys' first cousin—and the twenty-three year-old daughter of the man Frank Beran killed.

All four boys moved in with Rosie and her husband, where they were treated as sons. John, Benny, and Ernest were deemed old enough to work, and the Symm Family owned some fields. A young boy was a perfect size for picking cotton. A good crop grew about thigh high on a grown man who would have to constantly bend at the waist or knees to retrieve the bolls. However, a boy could stroll up and down the rows with relative ease, plucking the snowflaked buds from an upright position.

During late summer and early fall, this is precisely what the Beran brothers did from the time school ended until the sun no longer lit the fields, breaking only briefly on any bare patch of dirt to eat and drink. Thirty-five cents was their wage for every 100-pounds of cotton they pulled. After their first full summer in 1928, the boys' hands were so stained from the plants, it would be at least four weeks into the school year before enough bathings wore off the brown grit.

As Walter grew older he spent more time watching his brothers in the field from the back porch or, on really hot days, from an inside perch near a window. At two he was not old enough to join them in the work, an advantage his brothers reminded him of often, but which he didn't understand. He only knew that the three boys he admired most and who'd been the only playmates he ever knew were in the fields, and he was not. Walter was allowed to join them only when Rosie delivered their lunch. If it had been up to him, he would have shadowed their every move, dirty hands and all.

In the late fall of 1928, scarlet fever found its way to The Grove and into Walter's small body. Rosie labored against the rash and fever with constant cold compresses. She held him through the aches, not knowing if he'd survive. Most children who contracted the disease were at least five years old. At only two, Walter had unfavorable odds. If he did survive, Rosie was certain he would be frail for the rest of his life.

Two weeks after the disease had been diagnosed, Walter was back to toddling about the Symm's house, with no signs of permanent damage. It was considered a miracle, perhaps born out of God's mercy. It had become uncertain whether Thelma Beran was ever going to leave the Waco hospital and whether Walter would officially become an orphan. If he couldn't have his parents, at least he still had his health.

There was still an issue Walter suffered from which hadn't been dealt with;: a birth defect that hadn't manifested itself until he developed finer motor skills. As Walter grew into a full-blown toddler — handling whatever stick, rock, and ball he could find — it was clear that he preferred to use his left hand. Residents of The Grove saw left-handedness as a sign of the devil.

From the time he was three years old, whenever Walter attempted to use his left hand for any task, he received a whack on top of that hand. If he was at home, that meant a slap from the hand of an adult. If at school, his teachers used a stick. In time, the adults of The Grove beat down Walter's instincts. However, throughout the remainder of his life, a reflex would occasionally take over and Walter would pass a pen or a coffee cup back and forth between hands for a few seconds until the years of exorcising kicked in.

Walter finally joined his brothers in the fields as a mousy-haired five-year-old who'd already grown a reputation for his stubbornness and wit. Despite his longtime desire to pick cotton alongside them, he quickly formed an opinion that the work and wages were not commensurate. Walter continued working in the fields because his brothers made him, but inside the wheels began turning. Momentum was aided by a tent show that came to town during the summer of 1931.

The Beran boys couldn't afford the tickets, so the older brothers stayed home on the night the tent was showing a film. Walter wasn't giving up so easily. He snuck out a window of the Symm's house and crept his way to the tent, where he found a crack in the canvas. He peaked through it and on the screen was a family sitting in the loveliest living room he'd ever seen. *That's the life for me!* he whispered to himself. From that moment on, Walter began dreaming up ways he would get out of The Grove and make something big of himself.

***

A couple months after Walter joined his brothers in the cotton fields, the Beran boys received the news that their mother was returning home. She'd been gone for over four years. The boys were told she was not fully recovered and might never be. Walter's two oldest brothers, John and Benny, moved back into the one room shanty with their mother. Walter and Ernest moved in with the Dube family, who had more space than the Symms and more means to raise the growing boys.

In the weeks following Thelma Beran's return, the boys saw that their mother's wounds were still festering. While she was with them in body, she was emotionally vacant except for an agony that seemed to never subside. Thelma would slowly improve as Walter ascended the ranks of grade school, but by then there was little she could do to change the person he was becoming or perhaps had already become. Lawrence Dube, grandson of the General Store's proprietor, had something to do with this.

Lawrence and Walter shared the same age, and for three years, a bedroom, in the Dube family's house. They were brothers immediately. There were curiosities they could explore together that alone would have introduced too much risk. In other words, the two could take the fall better than one. Both also appreciated money. Walter's appreciation sprung from necessity; Lawrence's from birthright. It was a combination bursting with possibilities.

A penny interested Walter, and Lawrence knew how to wrangle stacks of them. By the time Walter was seven, he was a regular hand at the family's General Store during summers. Not only did the job get him out of the cotton fields, but he also learned everything from ordering to stocking to the charge system by which locals purchased their wares. The knowledge made him as asset to the wealthiest family in town, which had it perks. More than that, the job placed Walter in the path of every other town resident with means. Soon, Walter was moonlighting with any side job available—except picking cotton.

The path from the General Store to the Dube's home passed the Symm's house. Young Walter made a habit of stopping by to say hello to Rosie, whom he still considered his mother. After a brief conversation on the porch steps and perhaps a sip of cold tea, Walter would say goodbye and then hold out his hand. "Gimme penny," he would demand. The strategy was often successful.

All was not work and wages. Between school and the General Store, Walter and Lawrence found plenty of time for trouble. Ingenuity came in handy here as well.

In front of the General Store was a bench where the old-timers sat and solved the world's problems. The Great Depression was a popular topic at the time, but perhaps more so was the topic of prohibition. Until Walter was nearly eight years old, the sale, production, and transportation of alcohol was prohibited across the nation. This incited the town of German Lutherans, who quickly found a solution. They called it home-brewing.

Around the bench, the old men would gather and spill their secrets. Little did they know that Walter and Lawrence were taking notes. Soon the boys had memorized the recipe—every ingredient of which was available in the General Store's stockroom. The only remaining question was location: where would they conduct the operation? The answer was obvious to Walter—the least likely place anyone would look.

Perched twelve feet up in the branches of an oak tree behind the store, the boys finalized their plan and sealed it with a handshake. Over the next two days they squirreled away the ingredients in their pants—yeast, dried malt extract, hops, and sugar—and transported them to their shared bedroom. Once their rations were complete, they commenced work in Mrs. Dube's kitchen while the adults were away, boiling the malt extract into a dark base, letting it cool, and then adding the water and yeast.

From there they moved the operation under the cover of night to the location Walter had suggested. They left the concoction hidden away and returned the following evening to scrape off the excess yeast and pour the mixture from a jug into two-dozen used bottles they'd managed to obtain. Finally, the sugar was added before capping the bottles and beginning the waiting game. They would leave the bottles there for several days to ferment a second time with the sugar mixed in. They vowed to one another not to return until the proper time so as to not turn anyone on to their stash.

It was dark when they eventually returned to partake of their reward. They could almost taste the foamy head they had seen the old men sipping behind a local barn. With a homemade candle for light, they ducked under the foundation of a building and crawled to their stash.

As they came upon the case of bottles, they were struck dumb. Nearly every cap had been removed.

Walter picked up an open bottle and used the candlelight to try to peer inside. It was no use. He then smelled the bottle. The little that remained was pungent. He picked up another bottle. Same thing. He looked at Lawrence, perplexed.

Lawrence picked up one of the two bottles still intact. He tucked a knife beneath its cap and pried gently. The bottle hissed like an angry snake as foam crept from the tiny opening. He shot a glance at Walter, who nodded eagerly. Lawrence pressed down on the knife with force and the cap shot into the air on the head of a great beer geyser.

Lawrence held the bottle from his face while Walter covered his. When Old Faithful had finally ceased, Lawrence shook the bottle to his ear. There was only a sip, which the boys shared in utter concession. Now they knew why the caps had come off. They hadn't been removed. Their brew had built up enough pressure to blow the caps off the bottles. They would later learn they had added too much sugar to the mix, but not by way of a second attempt.

As it turned out, they had been making more commotion than they realized. When two police officers arrived on the scene and demanded the boys show themselves, any plans of reattempting home-brewing were foiled — at least if they were going to use the same hiding spot: the crawl space of the St. Paul's Lutheran church.

To say it was a significant lesson in Walter's life would be misleading. While the boys had their tails whipped by Lawrence's father, the experience ultimately taught them the value of precision. They straightened up for a few weeks and let the dust settle, then they went back to being boys. They managed to stay off the radar for at least two more years, until they'd grown gutsy enough to steal an old farmer's truck and promptly crash it into a barn.

The boys' discipline this time included the town's version of indentured penance: working the old farmer's cotton harvest for free. To work for no pay was merciful, in truth, as the boys could never afford to pay for the property damage themselves in any reasonable amount of time. Nevertheless, it was no form of mercy Walter wanted any part of again. To take from him the financial reward of hard work—even if only for a harvest—was not worth any whimsical risk. He would learn a real lesson this time: mistakes cost money.

Walter's penance was symbolic of the town's significant influence in his upbringing. Without it ever being said, The Grove was as much Walter's parent as his own mother, and perhaps more so than her in the early years when she was unfit to raise him properly. Rosie played a major role in this, as did the Dubes, who couldn't have opted out even if they wanted to with Lawrence and Walter attached at the hip. There were also others who had taken more than a sympathetic liking to Walter—like the pastor and the police officers who were willing to let boys be boys when they could, or the farmers who regularly created jobs for Walter despite their own financial challenges, or the school Bishop who took Walter to task for taking advantage of another boy in a pocket knife trade.

One can only speculate what might have become of the Beran brothers — and especially young, impressionable Walter — if the people of the The Grove had left a widow and her sons to fend for themselves. It would not have been uncommon if such had been the case. To give to another during a season of such deficit was not expected. Some might even say it was irresponsible. Hard times abounded, and that's precisely what made it so affecting in Walter's life.

While he was often an audacious boy, the townspeople seemed to see it as a positive sign that he was normal. Perhaps he would still make something of himself, despite the disadvantages he was bestowed before he had a say. They didn't know the half of it. They didn't know that beneath the boyish exterior was a deep well. Walter was taking it all in, storing it all up. He would not forget the unconditional love and sacrifice of Rosie. Nor the unrequited hospitality of the Symms. Nor the grace given by the pastor, police officers, and school bishop. Nor the opportunities created by every resident of The Grove who offered him a job.

It was because The Grove cared for him when he could not care for himself that Walter's dreams turned into a personal conviction. As an elementary school boy, he knew his limits, but he also knew that someday he would grow up and become something more than a store hand in a small town. He dreamed of what that something would be. Whatever it was, he would work hard at it and make The Grove proud. He would serve others the way The Grove had served him.

***

When he started middle school, Walter moved back home with his mother and it was then the two became family for the first time. His brothers were also there and they took him under their wings as only older brothers can. Laziness was not tolerated, nor was complaining. As long as you lived under the Beran roof, you worked to provide for the family's needs. Walter didn't mind the contribution, but he didn't appreciate his brothers' style of leadership back then. In time, he would.

The summer after he turned thirteen, Walter persuaded his brothers to allow him to move fifteen miles away into a boarding house in Temple, Texas to attend school at Temple High. The school was known for producing great football teams and Walter believed he'd make a great player. Perhaps, he thought, football was his ticket out of The Grove.

The one caveat his brothers conveyed was that he still had to hold down a job to provide his own meals, and he had to send all surplus funds back home. Walter agreed, reluctantly.

In Temple, he shared a room with two roommates and worked part-time at a grocery store during the week. On weekends he sandwiched the funnies into the Sunday edition of the local paper and pumped gas at a Temple service station.

With fall came tryouts for the high school football team. Walter was the new kid on the block, but he believed his passion and determination on the field would win him a spot on the team. It was a good philosophy that failed in application.

After the first day of tryouts it was clear to Walter that his 5'4", 120-pound frame had no business on a football field. He set aside those hopes and joined the yearbook staff and the student body government.

In class, Walter worked hard to get rid of his German accent, fearing the other kids would make fun of "a squarehead kid from the cotton patches of The Grove," as he later recalled. It's hard to say whether it was a factor in Walter's acceptance at Temple High, because by this time he had become rather good at making friends. His quick wit and good nature were popular enough that they would eventually get him elected as junior class president.

Walter remained at Temple High all four years, but not in the local boarding house. When the war came to America in 1941, John, Benny, and Ernest enlisted in the Army and were soon gone, along with nearly every able-bodied young man in The Grove. Walter moved back home with his mother and for the two and a half years that followed, he worked as the man of the house should, and his mom attempted to return to full strength. She worked wherever a job was offered, sometimes three a day, and when she wasn't working she cooked simple meals (vegetable stews typically), and she washed their clothes with a washboard and a bucket of water. Her slow-but-steady progress was important because when Walter turned seventeen and the country was still at war, both he and his mother knew he had few options. To be more precise, he had two.

In the fall after his seventeenth birthday, Walter began classes at Temple Junior College. An Army recruiter paid the school a visit the following February and met with every young man who had not yet enlisted. When it came time for him to speak with Walter, he presented the youngest Beran boy with two choices: take a Spanish classification test that would determine his role in a stateside industrial job related to the war effort, or enlist in the Army and be sent overseas for training.

The stateside industrial jobs were predominantly held by single women or married women whose husbands were at war. A young man could hold such a job, but not if he wanted to keep his manhood. Walter enlisted, along with every other male student on the campus.

Within a week, he was in the Army reserves at Baylor University in Waco, approximately thirty miles from The Grove. He was told he would remain there for two years for "pre-engineering training," before being sent to military duty. Walter turned eighteen on April 20, 1944. Twenty days later, on May 10, he was shipped overseas to active duty. Two years had turned into three months.

The Grove, Texas

Young Walter

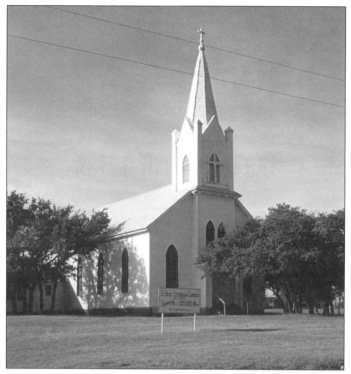

St. Paul's Lutheran Church, The Grove Texas

The Beran Home, The Grove, Texas

4

The Making of a Man

It was dark and drizzling outside when the cooks rose to begin preparing the turkeys and mountains of trimmings. Troops from three regiments of the U.S. Army's 66th infantry division were rounding their fourth week in a leased RAF camp on the outskirts of Dorchester, England. For the 2,000 soldiers — soft-skinned boys mostly, and few older than twenty-three — it had been a trying month. World War II was tearing through three continents, and of one fact each soldier was fully aware: at any moment they could be sent to the front lines of battle.

That knowledge made the downtime more tense than tranquil, especially since no one expected to stay put for so long. Many had come to feel that resting in a fog of uncertainty was worse than marching into the line of fire. They were ready to see action somewhere, anywhere. Just not on that week.

Christmas 1944 was only two days away. The air outside would remain damp and gray, but the large canvassed mess hall would be warmed by the sights, sounds, and smells of the season.

The mood was already lighter as the soldiers, including Private First Class Walter Beran, emerged from their barracks three hours after the cooks. Before long, most were sipping coffee, sharing cigarettes, and reminiscing about holiday traditions at home. Briefly, the war faded into the shadow of Christmastime's glow. Smiles wore easy. Conversations meandered freely, and in their midst a soldier slipped outside, donning his pack and disappearing into the nearby forest.

Few noticed he'd gone until he returned ten minutes later with the top half of a fir tree. No explanation was necessary. Two soldiers leapt from a bench and hunted a hammer and nails to fix the fir's trunk to the floor in the center of the hall. Walter caught on and dug up two bundles of thin rope. He and three others wrapped it around the tree's waist and then stretched it in opposite directions until each end found a suitable anchor. By this time, all present had gathered around the tree and claimed a task. Strips of gum wrapper foil were bent into loops to form a garland. Wadded red and green tissue paper became Christmas balls. Postcards from home and empty cigarette packs became colorful ornaments. And a tin can was cut into a star and rigged to the top of the tree.[1]

From somewhere in the crowd, a soldier began singing:
Now to the Lord sing praises,

All you within this place,

The others quickly found pace.

And with true love and brotherhood
Each other now embrace;
This holy tide of Christmas
All other doth deface.
O tidings of comfort and joy,
Comfort and joy
O tidings of comfort and joy

The songs and spirit prevailed into the afternoon as soldiers came and went from the mess hall to carry out their duties. Soon the scents from the kitchen monopolized the air and tapped at every belly.

It was early evening when everything changed.

Walter relaxed with his comrades around the wooden picnic tables flanking the Christmas tree. Known as the "short, square-jawed Texan,"

---

[1] Special thanks to Allan Andrade, American historical consultant for the 2009 National Geographic Channel documentary about the disaster "Deep Wreck Mysteries...Sunk on Christmas Eve", and author of *Leopoldville: A Tragedy Too Long Secret* (2008), and to Jaquin Sanders author of *A Night Before Christmas* (Macfadden-Bartell 1963) whose great work helped fill in some gaps in Walter's recollection of events.

he was only eighteen but he carried himself like a man two decades older. He was in the middle of sharing a small town tale when a large officer came through the main door of the mess hall. The man wore a serious expression on his face.

"Pack your things, boys. We leave for Southampton at 1900."

That was all he said, and then he turned and left through the same door in which he had come.

Suddenly, those who had been wishing for these very orders were in disbelief.

Now? Two days before Christmas?

Still, they were soldiers and this is what they did. Holidays were a wartime privilege, not a promise; even the best holiday of all.

There was an immediate and voiceless commotion in the hall: the squeaking and drumming of boots on the wooden floor, the clanking of tableware, and the rustle of rushing bodies pushing from the benches. Few were willing to make eye contact, as if doing so would crack the composure each knew he needed to maintain.

Questions ruled the mind of every young man as he made a quick path to his barrack and began assembling his pack, but the big question had been answered. The officer's countenance was a dead giveaway. They were being sent into battle.

As Walter arranged his personal effects, he wondered where he and his comrades were being sent. The thought of traveling led him to picture The Grove. He wondered how it had fared in the year he'd been at war, and wondered how his mother was managing without him. Just before he'd enlisted, the establishment of Fort Hood and the creation of Lake Belton had forced farmers and ranchers to forfeit some 300,000 acres of land. Many of them had to relocate, immediately changing the economic landscape of the town. Would he have a home to return to when the war was over?

One thing was certain: The Grove was no longer the town of his childhood, but it would always be home and it would always be the place where he learned to be a son, a brother, and a man. Still he wondered, as he did the other times he'd seen action, who he would be in battle. War made men of boys. It also made boys of men.

A small, leather-bound copy of the New Testament sat in the opening of his canvas pack. Walter reached down and held it in his hand. He didn't open it. Instead, he tucked it into his left shirt pocket.

He would read from it when they were closer to their destination. Its words would, as they always had, bring him a measure of peace amidst the swirling uncertainty.

***

At 7:00 PM on December 23, 1944, Walter and his fellow troops left Dorchester on a train headed to the port town of Southampton, England. There the 262nd and 264th Regiments of the 66th Infantry Division would board two ships to cross the English Channel to a port city in the lower Normandy Region called Cherbourg, France. No one knew that from Cherbourg the troops were to serve as reinforcements in the Battle of the Bulge, the United States' deadliest battle of the entire war.

The four-hour ride to Southampton was a quiet one, with most troops passing the time with their mouths and eyes shut. There was little to say, and few willing to say it anyway. They arrived at the docks in Southampton at approximately 11:00 PM to begin what would be a confusing and disorganized ten-hour boarding process. The two ships awaiting them were the *SS Cheshire* and the ship Walter would board, the *SS Leopoldville*.

By this time, the *Leopoldville* had serviced more than 50,000 soldiers of four different nationalities: Belgian ships' officers, Belgian Congo crew, British gun crew, and the Americans. Unfortunately, the ship's experience was no indication of the commanding officers' ability to lead an efficient boarding process. It wasn't until 2:30 AM on Christmas Eve that the soldiers finally began stepping onto the two ships. What should have been a quick and painless undertaking rapidly unraveled. The companies were split up and no one seemed to have an accurate manifest for the ships. As a result, few soldiers knew what ship they were to board. As the delay wore into the early morning hours, the officers began to assign soldiers to ships on the fly. The disorder only mounted aboard the *Leopoldville*.

The ship, which was a converted luxury liner, was only meant to accommodate 360 passengers. While it had fourteen lifeboats that could hold up to 799 passengers, the capacity was a far cry from the 2,235 soldiers that boarded her that night. The excess of bodies also meant tight and uncomfortable quarters. In some parts, hammocks and bunks were stacked four high. Morale was low and the soldiers couldn't help but complain about the state of their transportation.

As the ships finally pulled from the Southampton pier at 9:00 AM on Christmas Eve, no fire or abandon ship drills had been held on the *Leopoldville*, and no one knew how to lower the lifeboats. Furthermore, the diamond-shaped convoy, which included the *Cheshire* behind *Leopoldville* and the four escort destroyers — *Brilliant, Anthony, Hotham*, and *Croix de Lorraine* — did not have any precautionary antisubmarine reconnaissance. Worse still, the convoy's Commander John Pringle didn't know the exact number of soldiers he was charged with transporting.

Perhaps the officers assumed the Christmas spirit would protect them. Perhaps they were too tired to remember everything. Perhaps they were rushed and became negligent. Whatever the case, the convoy was finally (albeit clumsily) on its way to Cherbourg, France. The ten hours of confusion and chaos had at least kept the soldiers from picturing the battlefields where they would soon be standing. However, once the docks were behind them, they would have fourteen hours to imagine everything. For 764 of the young men, there would be less time.

At 2:30 PM, the *H.M.S. Brilliant* raised a black flag to signal to the *Leopoldville* that there was an unidentified object in the water. Alarms sounded on the *Leopoldville* and a few rushed to the deck and manned gun stations, but the majority of the soldiers were left to sleep, unaware of the potential threat headed their way.

An hour later, the *Brilliant's* sonar made three contacts that triggered depth charge attacks which felt like a small earthquake followed by a thunderstorm in the distance. Most soldiers below decks continued talking and sleeping as though nothing had happened. They would continue in this posture for the next two hours. For many, these would be the final moments of their lives.

The German U-boat *486* left its home in Kiel, Germany in mid-February of 1944 and eventually slipped into the English Channel undetected in the early fall. There, it waited for the right moment to fire. The *Leopoldville's* convoy was what German Lieutenant Gerhard Meyer had been waiting for. At approximately five minutes before 6:00 PM on Christmas Eve, the *Leopoldville* was five miles from the entrance of the Cherbourg harbor when Lt. Meyer ordered the launch of two torpedoes. Both hit the *Leopoldville's* starboard side.

The sound of the torpedo's impact was muffled beneath the water. A group on deck singing "Oh Little Town of Bethlehem" barely noticed the noise. They stopped singing for a moment and then resumed. The smell of gunpowder came soon thereafter and the *Leopoldville's* lights began flickering. Something had happened, but no one in the upper levels was sure what. Those who were sleeping closed their eyes again. Those who were eating picked their forks back up. Those who were carrying out their duties went back to work.

It was a different story in the lower decks. Private Beran had been sleeping in a hammock on the starboard side and was startled awake by the freezing water rushing through a massive hole in the side of the ship and rising fast. He shot upright and rushed for a ladder to climb to higher ground. Dozens of his friends and comrades were doing the same and it was difficult to resist clawing your way over the top of another. Nevertheless, honor prevailed as the soldiers pulled and pushed one another up the ladders, including those who were unconscious or had sustained injuries. Outside the ship's starboard side were lifeless bodies floating in the channel among the ship's debris. Some had been stripped naked from the force of the explosion. Yet only a few soldiers could see the gruesome wake of the torpedo strike, as darkness had already set in over the channel.

The *H.M.S. Anthony* was the first ship to realize the *Leopoldville* had been hit, some twenty minutes after the fact. The *Anthony's* Commander John Pringle radioed to Portsmouth, England, which was five hours away, because his radio (like all the Allied ships) was tuned to the frequencies used in England. The radio in Cherbourg, France, which was only an hour away, was tuned to a different frequency. Pringle then sent blinker signals toward the Cherbourg coastline where the French port was stationed. From the ship, one could make out the lights on shore.

Unfortunately, Fort L'Ouest, where the *Leopoldville* convoy was expected to arrive, hadn't seen a visible explosion. To make matters worse, the U.S. soldiers were at a Christmas party, including all of the senior officers, and those on duty had not only missed Pringle's blinker signals, they hadn't noticed that the convoy wasn't moving. It wasn't until Lieutenant Colonel Lee noticed the *Leopoldville* was off course and his subsequent messages to the ship went unanswered that rescue boats were sent. By this time, nearly thirty minutes had passed and it would take them another two hours to reach the damaged ship. The *Leopoldville's* fate would be sealed by then, as would the fates of those aboard.

Meanwhile, rescue efforts continued in the channel. The British escort destroyer *Brilliant* pulled to the *Leopoldville's* port side. The sea swell was causing a rise and fall between eight and twelve feet, making a clean leap from deck to deck impossible. Soldiers began climbing down the scrambling nets hanging off the *Leopoldville's* port side and then jumping to the *Brilliant's* upper starboard deck, some from elevations of 40-feet, breaking limbs as they landed. Other soldiers missed the *Brilliant* entirely and were crushed in the water between the two ships.

On the damaged side of the ship, Walter and two-dozen of his fellow soldiers had finally reached the ship's main deck. With several stairwells flooded or crushed, and with the prospect of carrying the bodies of the injured and dead with them, it had taken the group well over an hour. As they were caring for their wounded comrades any way they could, Walter looked up and spotted a sergeant. He rushed up to him.

"What do we do?" Walter blurted out.

"Wait until the last possible moment," the officer replied calmly, "and then jump and swim like hell."

Walter ran back to his fellow soldiers and reported what the officer said. The group immediately slipped their Mae Wests over their heads and then checked each others' to be sure they would perform. Once the vests were secured, the healthy continued preparing the injured for the plunge as best they could, while inside they all prepared to die.

The water temperature in the channel was in the mid-forties, making survival for more than a couple minutes unlikely. Each man knew this fact and wondered how quickly death would come. Their worries were accelerated as the ship began listing. All knew it was now only a matter of time. Soon there would be nothing left of the ship to stand on. They would have to enter the frigid water. If it was their time, this was how they would die.

Walter huddled tightly with approximately two-dozen other soldiers as the ship began to sink. No one spoke. They just stared at the dark, wet tomb surrounding them.

Walter's mind flashed to a picture of his mother's face. Tears welled in his eyes at the realization that she'd be forced to suffer another loss. Her baby, and the last of her boys to go to war, would be the first to die.

The heartache still lingered when the officer's abrupt command came. "Jump!"

Walter leapt into the icy channel alongside his comrades. Some jumped limply and landed too close to the ship. They were pulled into the vacuum created by the sinking vessel, unable to return to the surface in time. The moment Walter hit the water, he too was caught in the downward pull. Deeper and deeper he sank until finally he closed his eyes in surrender. Suddenly, his Mae West engaged and yanked him to the surface. He met the air with a huge gasp and immediately began swimming toward the lights of a small vessel in the distance. After fifty meters, he blacked out.

***

French fishermen returning to Cherbourg from a long day at sea had heard the muted torpedo explosion. They immediately turned around and headed toward the convoy well ahead of the rescue boats. Unfortunately, their fishing vessel was not made for speed. While they were the first to arrive on the scene, by the time they entered the field of destruction, there appeared to be no survivors. The only movement came from the swells of the channel rhythmically pushing the field of bodies and debris up and then down, up and down.

The fishing boat's captain continued guiding the vessel slowly through the wreckage nevertheless, swiveling his spotlight on the water for any sign of life. Suddenly, a fisherman pointed to something. It was a body floating face up. In the spotlight one could see a small cloud of vapor rise every few seconds from the mouth. The captain turned the tugboat toward the body until his men could reach it. They pulled the body onto the deck and looked it over. The face was cold and blue. The limbs were limp and rigid. The only effects on the body were the dog tags around the young man's neck and a small New Testament protruding from his left shirt pocket.

***

Shortly after the tragedy, the War Department sent out telegrams to families of the soldiers who died in the *Leopoldville* attack. The telegrams incorrectly identified the soldiers as "missing in action." The Germans had tipped off the AP News Agency that the ship had sunk, but the Army pre-empted the media and told the families their sons were missing in the European area, unrelated to the accident. This was likely to protect the fragile morale on the home front, which might not withstand the news of such a devastating loss.

French locals found bodies of *Leopoldville* victims washed ashore in January 1945, but the authorities told them not to broadcast what they found. Not even one French newspaper covered the catastrophe or any single, grisly discovery. British and American military authorities filed investigative inquiries away, marked "Secret." Fifteen years later, in 1959, the National Archive documents on the *Leopoldville* were declassified, but by then the event had largely been forgotten. What is known today is that 764 U.S. soldiers aboard the ship died from injuries sustained from the initial torpedo blast, hypothermia, or drowning. Somehow, for some reason, PFC Walter Beran was not one of them.

On the morning of Christmas Day, 1944, Walter awoke in a French military hospital to his own voice screaming, "Get me to land! Get me to land!" When he opened his eyes, a beautiful French nurse was standing above him offering reassurances that he was safe. For a moment Walter thought he was in Heaven and the nurse was an angel standing over him. Then he remembered the ship and the sinking. However, he recalled little about the icy waters of the channel and his questions for the nurses could not be answered. They knew only that he was in a hospital near the coast of Cherbourg, France and not, as he would later discover, on his way to the Battle of the Bulge, which would take the lives of ninety-percent of his regiment.

Five days later, Walter was released and transferred to the Brittany-Loire area where the other survivors from the 66th were stationed.

On December 29, 1944, the U.S. Army relieved its 94th Division in the Brittany-Loire area whose job had been to contain the enemy in St. Nazaire and Lorient by "carrying out daily reconnaissance patrols, limited objective attacks, and the maintenance of harassing and interdictory fires on enemy installations." By New Years Day 1945, the 66th Division had assumed full responsibility of St. Nazaire and Lorient.

The *Leopoldville* survivors were issued new clothing and they were given World War I 03 rifles because their own M1 rifles had been lost in the torpedo attack. The replacement rifles were filled with a rust preventative called cosmoline, which had to promptly be cleaned out. To make matters worse, the rifles could only shoot one bullet at a time, which put the soldiers at a great disadvantage. However, they would soon discover there was little to worry about. The area to which they were assigned had been effectively abandoned by the enemy as Germany mounted what would be one of its last major offensives many miles to the east in the Ardennes region of Belgium.

Days in St. Nazaire and Lorient were largely uneventful. The entire division was stationed across the river from a small town and given instructions that the town was off-limits. When evening arrived, the instructions were forgotten. After dinner and duties were finished, the soldiers crossed the bridge and descended on a local tavern. There they did what weary soldiers must do in wartime—everyone, that is, except Walter.

On the second night across the river, he took note of a dark-haired French woman in her seventies whom they passed along the way to the tavern. She was sitting alone at a table inside a small cafe. A single glass of wine sat in front of her. Walter couldn't forget her.

Once his buddies had some beer in their bellies, Walter snuck out the door and backtracked two blocks to the small cafe. The woman was still there and still sitting alone when Walter pushed opened the door and introduced himself. She stared at him a moment and then nodded knowingly to convey that she knew he was an American soldier. She then asked Walter to sit. As he did, she stood and retrieved another glass, which she filled with the same red wine she was drinking. She set the glass down in front of Walter and retook her seat and they began to talk, he in broken-French and she in broken-English. They talked as well as they could, and it was more than enough. When Walter stood, two hours had passed and he needed to hurry to catch his comrades. He thanked the old woman with a handshake. Though neither had time to say it, an unlikely bond had been formed that spurred an even more unlikely tradition.

Every night thereafter, as his comrades burned the path to the tavern, Walter slipped away to the old woman's cafe where they would share a new conversation and another glass of wine. The other soldiers soon caught on to Walter's detours and while they didn't understand them, they never let out the secret. The unauthorized ritual continued for more than four months until the Germans surrendered in May of 1945.

On the 66th's final night in France, Walter shared a last glass of wine with the old woman. They sipped slowly and spoke fondly until it came time to part ways for good. As Walter stood, the old woman reached out and grabbed Walter's hand. With small tears in her eyes she asked him for two promises if he survived the war: that he would buy a home with a garden to meditate on the events of life—"Men no longer do this," she said—and that each time he drank wine he would leave a swallow in the bottom of the glass to remember her.

Walter nodded. Then he embraced her and went on his way.

18 year old Army Private
Walter Beran

The Sinking of the Troup Ship Leopoldville ,
Christmas Eve 1944

5

Stealing Love

After the war ended in Europe, Walter's regiment remained over-seas until mid-summer on occupation duty in Zell am See, Austria. The general stationed there had been sent far more troops than he could occupy with duties. To give the surplus troops something productive to do with their time, he created the Rainbow University, which offered an array of courses like engineering, medicine, accounting, and language arts, among others. Walter chose an accounting course, figuring his countless hours at the E.W. Dube General Store might give him a leg up.

In late July, Walter completed his accounting course and then headed back to the States to earn an accounting degree at Baylor University. He quickly discovered he was well ahead of the freshman curve. A month into classes, his professor pulled him aside after class and proclaimed him to be the most brilliant accounting student he'd ever taught. Walter didn't tell the professor he was using the same book they studied in Zell am See, Austria. Walter allowed the compliment to fuel his confidence, nonetheless. That's not to say Walter was an exceptional student. While he excelled in accounting and made his grades elsewhere, he ultimately had his highest sights set on another subject: the opposite sex. In particular, one woman had caught his attention. Her name was Annette; a petite, outgoing brunette with whom he shared a history class.

Three weeks into the semester, Walter approached her after class one afternoon. He introduced himself and then struck up a conversation about taking her on a date. Annette was cordial and secretly affected by Walter's confidence and charm, but she felt the need to clear the air. She confessed she was already engaged.

"What's the hurry?" Walter shot back.

From that moment on he never called Annette anything but "Speedy." He also never asked her on another date. Instead, Walter took a different route. Every chance he got, he joined Speedy and her friends for ice cream or a movie or a stroll around the campus. His presence was subtle, but consistent. His strategy was simple, but effective. He would let Speedy get to know him and grow comfortable with him, without actually asking her to break the trust of her engagement.

Over Christmas break Speedy headed home to her hometown of Poteet, Texas, thirty miles south of San Antonio with a population of 1,200. It was there she did some reconsidering. In a matter of two days, it was clear that her heart had betrayed her. It was also clear that she didn't mind. Without a promise from Walter or so much as a conversation, she broke off her engagement in hopes something would bloom between her and Walter.

She returned to Baylor after the New Year with high hopes, but she began to worry when several weeks passed without a single sighting of Walter. The two no longer shared a class and he had not sought out her or her friends. Speedy wondered if he was still enrolled at the university. If not, she'd made a big mistake. Then the two spotted each other at the weekly campus chapel service.

Walter approached and, without a greeting, spoke frankly.

"Let's go get drunk."

Speedy paused as her eyes widened.

Then she grinned.

"Okay."

She would later admit to her friends that she was glad it was all he asked her to do because she would have gone along with anything he suggested. She had fallen for him the moment they first met, but there were reasons then to remain silent. Those reasons had been removed—all but one.

No one knows what actually happened on that first date and whether they actually followed through with Walter's proposition. The couple never told as it was against school policy to consume any alcohol, let alone consume enough to get drunk. However, one thing did become clear. The evening went well.

The two became inseparable, which was quite challenging at a private Baptist university during the 1940s. Besides the strict policy on alcohol consumption, there was a curfew to be upheld each night, limits on where boys and girls could fraternize, and a ban on public displays of affection. There were well-established ways around the rules that most of the students—not unlike Walter's comrades in France—were happy to keep secret whether or not they were in a relationship.

When spring break arrived, the couple planned to spend time together with both of their families. Their hometowns were only three hours apart and if they borrowed a car, they could split the break down the middle—half the time in Poteet and the other half in The Grove. There was only one problem.

Speedy was embarrassed to introduce Walter to her family. Despite the fact that her father owned a Ford dealership, she believed they were much too simple for Walter's kind. Walter hadn't said so, but he worried about the same thing. He had described his mischievous boyhood in the Dube household and general store. He hadn't yet disclosed the shack, the shooting, or the circumstances that followed.

Speedy didn't worry that Walter would treat her differently after meeting her family, but that he would think of her differently. Worse still, she worried that he would conclude they were from two different worlds that were not compatible in the long run.

She held these thoughts in her gut as the couple slid into the front seat of a friend's Ford and began the three-hour drive to Poteet. At Baylor, they primarily talked about classes and life on campus, largely benign topics. Away from Baylor, the doors opened to discuss everything else. Walter dove in and asked Speedy about life in Poteet. What was it like growing up there? She answered in affirmatives and generalities. Growing up in Poteet was good—it was like, she imagined, growing up in most small Texas towns. Her parents were good people. Like most, they were hardworking and made certain to instill in her the mores of good character and stewardship.

Walter's questions became more specific. He meant nothing but to show interest and ultimately set the stage for his own confessions. Speedy could feel her hesitation. Guilt rose in her gut.

Walter noticed and the full truth came out. He told her about the cotton fields and the tiny, one-room house in which he and his three brothers lived with their mother. He told her about Lawrence and about the barn crash and the famous home-brewing attempt. To Walter's delight, Speedy was in stitches. Then she asked about his father. His father, Walter said, "wasn't around."

There was an awkward silence. A giggle finally broke the ice.

"I've been worried about what you'd think about me once you met my family," Speedy admitted.

Walter grinned.

Then Speedy filled in her details.

Her family was not wealthy either. Her father was not an oil tycoon nor her mother a blue-blooded heiress. They lived a modest life in the same small house where she grew up. She had a pony that she loved as a girl and she used to ride it in shows. She still loved horses and didn't mind a little dirt on her clothes.

Walter laughed and shot Speedy a look that said, "That's just fine with me."

While their initial worries were put to rest on the drive to Poteet, there was another issue to which neither had given any thought. Speedy had been raised a teetotaling Southern Baptist. Walter had been raised a home-brewing German Lutheran. It didn't take long for the divide to become tangible.

On their first night in the Lott's home, Speedy's father did what any good father does; he peppered Walter with questions, to which Walter responded swimmingly. Or so it seemed. On the on the subject of drinking alcohol, there was no answer for Mr. Lott but total abstinence. Walter felt no need to hide his views as he had been brought up under Martin Luther's banner of impartial love, abundant grace, and "everything in moderation."

Walter gave a good report to Speedy of his exchange with her father. However, later that evening when Walter had slipped into the kitchen to speak to Mrs. Lott, Speedy learned the full report from her father, which greatly emphasized Walter's view of alcohol. Mr. Lott leaned in with a furrowed brow and muttered, "He's just like a damn Catholic."

***

They say when you make the choice to marry someone you're making the choice to marry her family as well. Mr. Lott made it known to Speedy that he was unhappy with her choice in men, but when it came time to speak, he held his tongue. Walter knew of Mr. Lott's disapproval because Speedy did not hide it from him. This pleased Walter, that she did not tuck away the friction in the name of hospitality. He loved her more for it. And besides, he was never deterred by a challenge. Now he knew she was not either.

Speedy was no southern debutante. She was one of three daughters born to a daddy who wanted a boy. He didn't get one, so he raised his girls to drive trucks and ride motorcycles, but his heart was still soft toward them. On one occasion, Mrs. Lott approached Speedy to give her a good spanking for something she'd done. Speedy ran out the front door and scurried under the house to a spot where her mother couldn't get to her. When her dad got home from work he was promptly sent after her. When Speedy saw her dad crawling under the house toward her, she exclaimed, "Is she after you, too?"

Mr. Lott burst into laughter and Speedy avoided her spanking. That's not to say Mr. Lott wasn't tough when he needed to be.

When Speedy was five and with her dad on a nearby ranch, she spotted a Spanish pony named Dolly that she couldn't live without. It wasn't expensive, but Mr. Lott wasn't one to splurge.

"Daddy!" she exclaimed. "Can I have it?"

"If you can get the pony home," he replied, "she's yours."

She was thrown three times on the way, but Speedy got herself and that pony home with every bone intact.

Speedy was an unexpected tomboy—a petite, pleasant-faced young lady who stood just over five feet tall—a daddy's girl who was as strong-willed and as capable as she was well-mannered. The same traits freed her up to become her own woman, which included what she would later call a "Southern Lutheran view" of alcohol that fit well with any native of The Grove. It also included a touché geared toward Walter, who had so deftly nicknamed her Speedy.

When she returned to school after the summer of 1946, Walter was mapping out a time and place to propose. He got her alone and presented her with a box that contained a ring he had designed himself—with a paperclip and a pea. Speedy looked down at the ring. Then back up at him. Then back down at the ring. Then back up at him.

"Will you marry me?" Walter asked.

Before she had to answer, Walter grinned, withdrew the paperclip and pea, and pulled the real ring from his pocket. Speedy heaved a sigh, and said yes. It was then she let forth a secret.

"I've always wanted to marry a Barry," she confessed. From that day forward Walter was her "Barry." She never explained the odd affinity other than to say it was a name she had been drawn to since she was a small girl. It didn't matter to Walter, who figured that if Annette had no problem with him calling her Speedy, he could put up with being called Barry.

Two years passed as weeks while the engaged couple continued their schooling at Baylor. Walter no longer had a need to ask for dates, as both assumed they wound spend every spare moment together, despite the rules. Speedy was as willing as Walter to find creative ways to be together. There were group dates, as they were easiest, and Walter grew to know Speedy's girlfriends quite well. There were also a few toasts on special occasions. Three or more was a crowd from time to time.

Graduation finally neared in the spring of 1948 and Speedy was at work with her mother planning a simple wedding in her hometown. Then on May 28, 1948 Walter "Barry" Beran and Annette "Speedy" Lott were married. Walter's mother and Rosie Symm's mother—the widow of the man Walter's father had killed—drove to Baylor where they picked up the couple and returned them to Poteet for the wedding. Mr. Lott gave his daughter away and a young Baptist preacher married her and Walter in the First Baptist Church. Thankfully, Speedy's father had determined that Lutherans could be enjoyed in moderation.

After everyone had their fill of punch and wedding cake, the newly-weds borrowed Mrs. Lott's Ford coupe and (with a hundred dollar bill from Speedy's father) drove to the St. Anthony Hotel in San Antonio where they spent one night overlooking the downtown park. The next day they woke, ate breakfast at the hotel restaurant, and then returned to Waco for Walter to finish out the final month of his college degree. The truncated honeymoon was not a surprise—the couple knew it was the price of not waiting until after graduation. However, the one-day honeymoon was also a subtle sign of the days ahead. Walter had always been a driven boy, able to chase down his own needs and desires. Now he was a man with the needs of two on his plate and an abundance of bigger desires. College had been a nice break. His marriage and career would not be seen in the same light.

The forty-five year-old, Cleveland-based accounting firm Ernst & Ernst was the first company of its kind to recruit future employees from college campuses. They'd paid Baylor a visit in the late spring of 1948 and offered Walter a job at their San Antonio offices upon graduation. Walter accepted and he and Speedy found a cheap, furnished apartment to rent until they could save some money and find a nicer place. While Walter worked regular hours during the day, Speedy did her best to make some friends, but apartment living wasn't very conducive to it. After a month of doing little but waiting on Walter to come home each day, she joined a women's bridge club that introduced her to some local wives her age.

Meanwhile, Walter was growing leery of his new job. He didn't mind the work, but he found himself increasingly wondering what else was out there. He wanted to own a piece of something one day and at an older company like Ernst & Ernst, this seemed unlikely. After nine months, he gave his notice.

He called up his older brother John, who was a manager in the grocery store business, and found work as a bagger in one of his Katy, Texas stores. Two months later he'd learned all he needed to know: grocery stores were a family business that he would never get a piece of. Walter returned and begged his old job back if for no other reason than because Ernst wasn't a family business and it offered more opportunity to travel than a grocery store.

Whether he was thoroughly convincing or the top brass felt sorry for him, Walter never said, but Ernst & Ernst rehired him. The commitment he displayed from that day forward was, if anything, to avoid proving his boss a fool and himself a fraud. His application of one particular strategy bode well to both ends.

A few months into his second stint at Ernst, Walter noted that the firm occasionally let an employee go after a project was completed. Walter quickly formed a habit of never alerting the top brass that a project he was working on was finished. He simply jumped aboard the next project.

He also formed a habit of studying the tax laws religiously. Right after he returned to the firm, Congress passed a major change, which few understood. Soon, whenever someone in the office had a question about the new law, the common reply was, "Go ask that new kid. He knows everything about it."

Erwin Heinen was a mentor of Walter's in the early days and one of the first to take note of Walter's upside. Heinen would go on to take charge of Ernst's Houston office, but he never forgot the impact that young Walter Beran had on him. Years later, he said that he knew Walter was "a real comer" with a "beautiful ability to handle all classes of people, from the janitor to the head of the company. He was good at dealing with clients and employees, and he was active in the community. The manager of an office has to be a good public relations person, as well as being technically sound and a good administrator. The other thing that stands out about Walter was his sense of diplomacy. He was able to see the client's point of view, which sometimes conflicted with the firm's. He was very calm; he didn't get ruffled easily. At the same time, he exuded enthusiasm. He's always been a people man. He knew how to make people happy—even when they were mad at him."

John Carden, an Ernst employee who would eventually serve under Walter, once gushed that he was "amazingly well-balanced. I got tremendous perspective and experience from working with Walter," continued Carden. "It's not that he acted as a rabbi, but he had a very real influence. I've tried to emulate those things he stood for—decency, sincerity—and to take the time to stop and care. He had an enormous appetite for work; very few people could keep up with his pace. There were certain stock phrases he used to keep things in perspective: 'Keep it cheerful and friendly,' was one of them. When he wanted to point out the absurdity of some trivial concern, another favorite was, 'In 50 years, we'll all be dead.'"

There was more to Walter's commitment than simple survival. His dreams in the cotton fields hadn't left him. He was indebted to a world that had helped him beyond tragedy, out of poverty, and around death. He had no excuse not to make something of himself, and in doing so reciprocate the grace and goodness he'd been shown.

The Berans moved into an apartment in San Antonio and Walter wasted no time making his mark. This was an accounting job after all, and he'd been in that business since he was five. Life, it seemed, was quite simple if you knew what you wanted and how to get it. The Grove and Lawrence Dube taught him that. Walter had his woman, a borrowed car through her dad, and now a steady job. What he didn't have was furniture.

The Berans owned nothing they could use in the new apartment—not a couch or desk or chair, not even a bed. It was hardly a romantic atmosphere, let alone one suited for the family they hoped to start. Upon hearing of his best friend's plight, Lawrence Dube secured a mattress from his family that they could borrow and then managed to hit up a few others in The Grove for anything they could spare. Walter picked up Lawrence and a trailer full of furniture and drove it to the apartment in San Antonio. The set up was neither attractive nor warm, but it was enough. They had somewhere to sleep, and attend to other matters. Speedy was pregnant within a matter of months.

While Walter was busy with work one weekend, she drove home to break the good news to her parents and sister. After she'd told them and they'd exchanged hugs, the three women began talking about their husbands' ancestry and wondering whose features the coming child would have.

"Barry is German-Czech," explained Speedy.

Mr. Lott overheard. "I damn sure wouldn't brag about it," he added.

In August of 1951, Speedy and her beloved German-Czech welcomed their first son John into the world. Shortly thereafter, the young family moved into their first house on Lark Avenue. In December 1953, Walter and Speedy's second son James (a.k.a. "Jim") was born.

***

On the outside, the 1950s was a decade of growth for the Berans, as it was for many American's who basked in the wake of post-war prosperity. Anything could be had for those who were willing enough. Walter's responsibilities expanded as quickly as he could manage them into his schedule and he was earning the rewards of his hard work—small promotions and with them, small raises that eventually allowed him to purchase a car and allowed Speedy to properly adorn their home. This new decor came in handy as her friendships with the neighboring women grew and the Beran household became a place of congregation.

Nearly every day Walter was at work, Speedy would have her girlfriends over for bridge. Those who had children brought them along and John and Jim did their best to entertain them, which is to say they used the other children as entertainment. The boys' personalities shone through in this context. If you told John no, he stopped. If you told Jim no, he looked at you and promptly went back to work.

To make matters worse, Walter was a softy when it came to disciplining the boys, so using tough love to change Jim's ways was never going to be a united front. Back then it was always Jim who needed the discipline. Speedy was determined and consistent. She would spank Jim and send him to his room when he misbehaved. Then the weekend would come and Walter would do nothing but laugh at the stubbornness of his son and bribe him into compliance with an ice cream cone or a piece of candy. John stayed out of trouble by comparison, but he was watching his younger brother work.

At a glance, the Berans' life seemed to embody the American Dream. Gainfully employed father; happily equipped mother; two healthy, energetic boys with a yard out back and an aluminum boat to explore the nearby river and fish from its banks. In many ways, it was an accurate depiction.

Walter and Speedy were in love; they had a clean, hospitable home; and now they had two growing reasons to celebrate their lives together. To the naked eye, the only downside was that Walter's workload had him gone more than anyone liked. In fact, the father of two boys who lived next door saw little John and Jim so often they called him "Daddy" for a season until Walter heard about it and set them straight. Occasionally, Walter and Speedy sat on the couch after the boys were asleep and shared a glass of wine and dreamed about their future. They'd start with their dreams for the boys and for Walter's work and inevitably the dreaming would end up on what life might look like when the boys grew up and were on their own. Speedy would be content, she said, if nothing about their circumstances changed and they all had their health into old age. Walter was more precise.

He'd begun collecting books that he planned to sit down and enjoy one day: fiction, poetry, and the complete works of any particular author with whose philosophies Walter shared some common ground. He'd also begun collecting bottles of fine wine to enjoy alongside his books. His strategy was simple. Each glass of wine he drank was like an audit of its bottle. If he enjoyed the taste, he recorded the name and vintage and he bought a bottle to store at home. If he didn't enjoy the taste, there was no harm done. Either way, every glass still afforded him the opportunity to remember the old French lady. He always left the last swallow at the bottom.

The Berans seemed to be leading a charmed life. Through a microscope: there's more to it than what it seems.

Just before the birth of John, Walter was diagnosed with what the doctor called a "weak heart." In layman terms, this meant his heart was not pumping as much blood as it should. The doctor's prognosis was somber. Walter would not live a long life. His heart would "give out sooner than most." Walter asked at what age this would occur. The doctor would not predict an age, but he asserted that Walter would likely not see his fifties. In other words, Walter Beran's life—at twenty-five years old—was already half over. That was the doctor's best prognosis.

When Walter told Speedy the news, he ended the conversation with an assertion.

"God has kept me alive thus far and he will keep me alive as long as there is good work to be done. Whether I live another ten years or seventy, my days are numbered by Him, and Him alone."

The display of faith brought Speedy comfort. She believed, as Walter did, that God could keep him alive for another 100 years if He desired to. Still, the diagnosis remained in the back of her mind, just behind another more tangible concern.

The traumas of war had caught up to Walter. Once a month, he woke in a pool of sweat, screaming for his mother. Speedy shook him awake each time and kept her hands on his body until his heart slowed. He walked to the bathroom to rinse his face. Then he changed shirts and returned to bed in silence.

When Speedy attempted to address the nightmares, Walter put an abrupt end to the conversation. The war was not a topic he wanted to discuss then or ever. It was behind him, thank God, and he preferred it to stay that way. Speedy understood. She also worried that the nightmares were only the tip of the iceberg.

By this time she knew about the whole story of Walter's father, Walter mother Thelma Beran had come to live with them on Lark Avenue when John was born. Had she not known of Thelma's past, she would have simply labeled her moody. However, Speedy knew enough details about that day in 1927 that she sympathized with her failure to fully recover from her emotional wounds. Grandma Beran was helpful with John and Jim, but having her in the home was a constant reminder that Walter was not unscathed either. For this reason, Thelma's passing in 1958 of natural causes was met with mixed emotions in Speedy's heart.

She shed genuine tears of sorrow for the loss of her daily companion, the boy's grandmother, and her husband's mother. She also felt relief that Thelma's burdens had come to an end and so had the daily reminders of the vulnerability in Walter's armor. Speedy thought Thelma's death would distance Walter from his childhood in a healthy way. Such was the case, for precisely twenty months.

In the winter of 1960, Walter received a call from the Austin State Hospital. His father had died in his sleep. The news seemed to resurrect a demon in Walter's psyche: he was essentially an orphan with no one to fall back on. The old voice now announced that he was officially one.

Two days after receiving the news, Walter informed John and Jim that their grandfather had died. They didn't understand at first. It was the first they'd ever heard of having a grandfather on their dad's side. Walter had told them nothing of 1927. To that point he'd only said that their grandfather was "gone." The boys assumed it meant he was dead. When Frank Beran was truly gone, Walter knew it was time to tell the boys the truth—not the exhaustive history, but simply that their grandfather had been living for the past thirty-three years in a hospital for people with mental illness, a place he had visited only a handful of times. Now their grandfather was dead.

It was a heavy load to drop on the boys all at once. It affected John the most. At nine years old, he was able to comprehend the news and attempt to field the weight of it.

Sensing this, two days after his father's death, Walter took John with him to Austin where they lay Frank Beran's body to rest in a local cemetery. For reasons he never explained to anyone, Walter chose not to transport his father's body to The Grove to be buried alongside his mother. Instead, he said his goodbyes in a city cemetery near the state hospital with his oldest son beside him. Then he walked to his car and drove back home to San Antonio.

Walter offered few details of the trip to Speedy when he and John returned. If he felt any deep emotions he didn't share them, at least not verbally. He simply returned to his work, and life carried on as it had before.

In the days and weeks that followed, there was no tangible difference in Walter's posture. He was not suddenly aloof, nor was he suddenly intense. The only notable change was that his work responsibilities steadily increased. Or perhaps Walter increased them.

What began as a predictable, nine-to-five job quickly became an all-hours-as-needed job. Ernst was rapidly expanding and there was an opportunity for Walter to ride the wave if he could keep pace. His instructions were simple: be more than a bean counter. It suited Walter fine. While numbers came naturally for him, he had always seen himself as a business consultant or better yet, an advocate for his clients' financial futures. Now he was being encouraged to position himself as such and offer the appropriate services—business accounting on the first tier and business advice and accountability on the second. He was equally adept at both and he leaned into the opportunity to expand his role in the company.

Walter stretched his travel as far as possible, quickly addressing issues with current clients and meeting with new prospects in his region. While he was continuously mindful of the increasing time he spent away from Speedy and the boys, he was equally mindful that their futures were in his hands. If he did not succeed in his work or if he merely became expendable, the fall was still not far to The Grove. His work success was the only insurance against regression and so he gave himself wholly to it. This included reading numerous books on time management and every good inspirational quote book he came across in his travels. It also included becoming a golfer.

After a few rounds, Walter quickly concluded that his stature and impatience were great disadvantages—not to mention his lack of directional skill, an expensive drawback when considering the number of errant balls he was forced to locate in the small forests flanking most fairways. After a particularly dreadful shot, Walter would often mutter, "Shit" under his breath and then immediately, "Forgive me, Lord." Walter's commitment to his career kept him playing—good business could be conducted on the golf course — but to make the game more bearable, he eventually made it more fun.

Early one morning at the San Antonio office, Walter created a special business card for his days on the golf course. He would hand them out whenever the time was right. He printed out 100 sheets on blue card stock then laminated and cut them himself. The cards were one-sided and each read as follows:

HOPE OPEN

ST. MULLIGAN'S INDULGENCE

Be it known to all that this indulgence, having been secured
by expenditure of currency, entitles the bearer to
total forgiveness of one errant shot.
No further guilt need be born nor sin tax will be exacted.
~ St. Mulligan

Walter was not unaware of the effect his commitment to his work would have on his family. He didn't want to leave them behind. In the early 1950s, he had commenced a habit of writing Speedy a letter each night he was away on business. His territory had just expanded outside Texas and included visits to cities he'd never seen before. He didn't know the full measure yet, but Walter was also joining a remarkable local group of current and future business leaders who would go on to become greatly successful. Many would also become longtime clients and friends. The group included Tom Benson of Tom Benson Chevrolet who would go on to become the owner of the New Orleans Saints, Howard Edward Butt, Sr. of the HEB store chain; H.B. Zachry of Zachry Construction, and Red McCombs, co-founder of Clear Channel Communications and later the owner of the Denver Nuggets, San Antonio Spurs, and Minnesota Vikings, a car dealership empire, and the namesake of the University of Texas Business School.

There was an excitement to experiencing the new frontiers with fellow pioneers and he wanted to share that excitement with Speedy as much as possible. Unfortunately, Walter caught a nasty bug a few weeks into his commitment to writing her letters, and he, discontinued the letter writing. He intended to pick it back up once he regained full strength, but the practice had lost its charm by the time he was healthy. He powered forward in the name of his family, but increasingly without them.

The saving grace for Speedy and the boys was their location. San Antonio was thirty minutes from her parents in Poteet. Furthermore, they were still in Texas and surrounded by likeminded southerners. By the end of the decade, the Berans had become a fixture in San Antonio. They had also moved to a bigger home on West Kings Highway.

In the fall of 1960, Ernst & Ernst made a move that Walter would later confess carried the odds of Buster Douglas knocking out Mike Tyson. A position opened up in the firm: partner in charge of client relations. Walter was given the job. Besides the shock waves that circulated the national offices, the promotion came with a significant raise and enormous responsibility. The company was putting its faith in Walter and he wasted no time making the company glad they did..

In the next partners' meeting, the chairman of Ernst raised a question about responding to the accounting opportunities the newly liberated health care industry provided. There were no standards or guidelines, he pointed out. "Who will set this standard?" he asked.

"We will," Walter shot back. In the subsequent weeks, he wrote the benchmarks upon which the company would build its healthcare accounting and consulting practice.

Despite the quick success, there was also an immediate downside to Walter's new position—a major uptick in travel throughout Middle America, which meant more time away from Speedy and the boys. Walter did his best to offset his absence. When he was home he took the boys on weekend trips, like the Rooke Ranch in Woodsboro, Texas for some serious deer hunting. The boys were more interested in arguing, exploring the 35,000 wooded acres, and eating hamburgers off the grill. They made memories, nonetheless. A few months later, Walter flew to Washington D.C. from Cleveland and met Jim's flight from San Antonio. The two spent three days touring the nation's capital and its surrounding sights.

Hovering over the memories was a gray cloud only Walter saw clearly. A conversation eventually ensued between he and Speedy during the summer of 1964. It would be better described as a "polite notification." There was never any doubt in Walter's mind that they would have to move to Cleveland, where the Ernst & Ernst national headquarters were located. He let Speedy know that the move was now imminent.

Speedy verbalized her support, but secretly she saw the move through a different lens than Walter's. While she found comfort and pride in his increasing success, she much preferred their San Antonio routine. She would have chosen to stay put over the raise. There was another underlying reason that she mentioned to no one.

The world was evolving more rapidly than Walter's career. Beneath the pinnacle of American prosperity during the Truman and Eisenhower presidencies were the rumblings of discontent and change. Amidst the swirl of emotions, the talk of a new kind of woman was emerging. While she supported equal rights, Speedy worried the new image of a woman would devalue the role she enjoyed the most, as a home-maker. She found great purpose in supporting Walter's work and in raising their two boys to make something great of themselves. On West Kings Highway she felt supported. She worried that might not be the case up north.

Speedy and Walter, Young Love

6

Roots

In August of 1965, Speedy and John spent three days in Poteet before flying northeast to meet Walter and Jim, who were pulling a trailer to Cleveland. Walter knew the time with her parents would renew Speedy's spirits, and that was needed. Ohio was another world—one with a fourth season called winter that wasn't merely brown. Only he had experienced snow firsthand.

In the weeks prior to the move, Walter had found a nice home on a quiet street called Lyman Circle in a family-friendly suburb called Shaker Heights. In the early 1960s, Shaker Heights boasted the highest per-capita income of any suburb in the U.S. Walter hoped the upscale locale and larger house would help Speedy acclimate quicker and provide some creature comfort to her and the boys.

It was a two-story brick home with room to spare and a back deck overlooking a big yard where the boys could play. A park and a library were a short walk away. He could not reason Speedy into excitement, so he would pamper her into it.

With nearly twice the square footage, the house felt like a mansion compared to West Kings Highway. Now, with enough money to fill it with furniture and modern appliances, Walter was certain Speedy would be surrounded by reasons to smile. On most days, she did. Inside, she held her judgment.

Years later Speedy would admit to a friend that she "hated Cleveland less than she had planned." It was her most honest assessment of the experience. It was also in hindsight. Had Walter not made the decision to reignite an old habit in the months leading up to their move, her experience might have more closely matched her expectations.

On September 16, 1964, Walter picked up a pen and sheet of paper and began writing letters to Speedy again. His strategy was different this time.

Instead of mailing the letters or simply delivering them in person upon his return, Walter asked his Ernst assistants Mary Jean and Rose to compile the letters in a large, green Naugahyde photo album accented with post cards, pictures, tickets, and other scrapbook items he collected along the way. The album—containing eighty-two letters spanning from September 1964 to October 1965—was presented to Speedy on her birthday: October 5, 1965.

In his letter introducing the album, Walter came clean about his original half-hearted attempt to write Speedy a note each night he was away. Then he was forthright about how and why he came to renew the commitment.

> *Cleveland, Ohio*
> *October 5, 1965*
>
> *It has been about a year ago now when one day I was again reminded of how peculiarly wired up we human beings are, and that I had long ago worn out the 1952 excuse not to write you a daily note while away. So, since that day a year ago, I have returned to the pre-1952 routine.*
>
> *What you will find in the pages to follow are my daily notes to you together with some odds-and-ends, mostly pictures of airports and motels. When I began them, I had a lot of ambitions—to write poetry, clever verses, sage advices, but as you will note, they well reflect the incongruities within me.*
>
> *My fond plan was to present this collection of notes and odds-and-ends to you during a party at the St. Anthony Club in San Antonio. Our close friends would have been present. That part of the plan had to be changed. But in spite of that change, it diminishes in no way the love and affection which inspired the notes which follow.*

*God has been good! Our blessings together have
been and are immeasurable! My task is to remain, if I
am, and to strive to be, if I am not, a credit to God, to
you, and to the precepts, which I confess. Yours is to
continue in the love and inspiration, which have been
mine for seventeen-plus years.*
    B.

    P.S. Ich liebe dich von ganzem herzen mit schmerzen!

"I love you so much my heart hurts," conveys the final line in English.
The album and its confession were just the elixir Speedy needed only a
few weeks into their move. Walter knew that following him there with
the boys in tow would be a far greater strain on her than anyone else
in the family. His travel and hours at the office would somewhat insu-
late him from life in their new town. Speedy would feel the full brunt
of the uprooting.

Walter hoped she'd grow roots again and he believed the letters
would remind her that no matter where they lived and whether they
were in each others' presence, they were united, and he was thinking
of her. Each letter said as much in its valediction. "I think of you often!
I miss you!" they all exclaimed before signing off with, simply, "B"
for Barry.

The letters also provided Speedy a clear window into Walter's
world—something she didn't have in San Antonio—and a window into
the world at large. It had changed a lot since they had met.

America was accelerating down a path called progress with problems arising from a populace who had increasingly less time to reflect
on where they were heading—a populace who had somehow shifted
from a spirit of reflection in the 1940s to a spirit of rebellion in the 1960s.

On July 7, 1965, Walter plainly observed, "People are always
coming and going." The trouble, he noted, was that progress had its
pros *and* cons. "Before we had no communications," he told Speedy.
"Now we have too many." The result was a growing epidemic of "traveling but not taking in," which inevitably produced "a feeling a numbness." Three days after penning the latter phrase to describe the people
he observed in an airport, he watched young soldiers—many of them
as young as he was when he joined the Army—boarding a plane that

would commence their journey to Vietnam to fight a war Walter couldn't understand. He wondered if the feeling of numbness had reached a perilous point. He also wondered if it had infected him.

Shortly after returning from that trip, Walter received a letter from a former Army comrade. The *U.S.S. Leopoldville* survivors from the 66th Infantry Division were planning a reunion and invited Walter to attend. The timing seemed providential and Walter jumped at the opportunity, offering to host the event at the Pine Lake Trout Club in nearby Chagrin Falls, Ohio. It was there, among those who understood him, that Walter finally allowed himself to talk about the war, and in particular the *Leopoldville* tragedy. It was the first time he'd spoken of it since the war. The evening served as a catharsis that reinforced his intentions to protect himself and his family from becoming casualties of progress.

Walter didn't wonder whether the letters were helpful to Speedy. He assumed they were and he continued writing with greater resolve. He was right about the letters' effect, and he was wrong.

When Walter was out of town, she would sit down after the boys were asleep and re-read her favorites. Walter's words and experiences helped Speedy find temporary legs in Cleveland. She was supporting a worthy cause—her husband's ascending career. He was working hard to provide well for her and the boys. Why should she complain?

However, as the white winter labored into February and March, and Walter ventured across the Midwest, Speedy's strength waned. The letters lost their luster. Compiled and presented at once, they were an undeniable testimony of love, respect, and devotion. However, as an anthology they were also a fading presence, like a family vacation or a birthday celebration.

The boys missed Walter's presence, too. They missed him in equal measure, but their difference in age made for different experiences with their yearnings.

Jim was not yet twelve. To him, time was still an arbitrary gauge. The passing of seven days was not much different than three or four. He was not hindered in making the most of every moment his dad was home. Nor was he hindered when he was away.

John was now a shaggy, blonde-haired teen and time had begun to mean something to him. An hour was an hour more and seven days felt like forever. The move to Cleveland had come when John was entering a season of doubt and self-discovery. By the time he was fourteen, his emotions had begun to manifest themselves in a growing mutiny. Walter was rarely around to witness it. He would only hear of it from Speedy upon returning from a trip. He then faced the choice of either excavating the matter from the past and administering belated discipline, or letting the sleeping dog lie. Either way was problematic.

For a season, it seemed the brothers had reversed roles. Jim was as capricious as ever, but he'd substituted his interest in outright rebellion with an enthusiasm for food that Walter called "a marvel to behold." John had assumed the rebellious role. The trouble was that Walter's role had changed, too.

He could no longer laugh at rebellion and divert it with bribes. The boys were old enough to know better, and they were smart enough to take advantage of him. For these reasons John was never allowed to enjoy a season of unrequited grace as Jim had when they were younger. John waited too long to rebel, and so when he did it was met with firm opposition rather than amusement. It wasn't fair as John saw it.

On a Saturday morning during early spring, John took matters into his own hands. He tucked away all his savings, some food, a change of clothes, and a few items for entertainment. Then he ran away. He stayed gone for as long as he could so as to make the greatest impact. That is to say he returned home once daylight faded and he'd run out of food and money. His actions still warranted a response—just not the one he expected.

Once Speedy had given him an earful, Walter escorted him into a back bedroom. John expected the belt. In his mind, nothing else would prove his voice had been heard. His dad had something else in mind.

Walter sat John down on a bed and expressed his sadness for what John had done. For the disrespect he'd shown for his mother's feelings. For the disloyalty he'd shown his family. Mostly, for the disregard he'd shown for his own life.

Walter explained to John that he'd be his own man soon and that his choices as a teenager would dictate what sort of man he could become. Walter placed his hand on John's shoulder. "But I want you to know," he concluded, "your mother and I love you and we believe in you." Walter then left the room. Nothing more was said about the incident.

The upheaval swirling inside John was a reflection of what he was witnessing all around him. This was the era of experimentation, free love, and asserting individual rights. The era of standing up for what you believed in. The trouble was that John didn't yet know what he believed in. He wanted to be seen and heard, but on what grounds he didn't know. Speedy had observed the result. Now Walter had, too.

Much to Walter's chagrin, his sons were growing up in a world full of philosophies that offered many questions and few definitive answers. As he saw it, the country no longer felt the sting of the Great Depression. It no longer found its strength in the unity of a war. The country was divided and had lost its footing. John and Jim were growing up, literally and figuratively, outside The Grove of Walter's boyhood.

Walter's world was full of enterprising possibilities through which he could more thoroughly repay his debt of gratitude. It was also a world of instability into which the boys could easily lose themselves. The faces of three young Mississippi civil rights' workers who'd been murdered in the summer of 1964, James Earl Chaney, Andrew Goodman, and Michael Schwerner, were still fresh in Walter's mind.

This dichotomy was a prominent theme in Walter's first album of letters, as was his take on the solution. Two letters in particular embody the essence.

November 9, 1965
...Crisis seemed to be the order of the day.
This morning's paper reported:

- *Fifty-eight killed in Cincinnati plane crash*
- *Eisenhower rushed to hospital*
- *Dorothy Kilgallen found dead*
- *Viet Cong ambushes battalion of Yanks*

...But the same paper had the following: "Our Father, when burdens and frustrations beset our lives, make us wise enough to lift our eyes above our plodding feet to the mountain peaks that remind us Thou art God."
So, as always, there's hope and basis for optimism.

November 22, 1965
Two years ago at noon today the world first learned of the tragic assassination of President Kennedy. It was an almost impossible thing to accept when...I first

heard of it at the San Antonio Club. It was proper for Ned Dunn the president of the club to assert, "This club is closed! Let's go home, get on our knees, and pray!"

Tonight I am in Washington and not too far from the White House, the last official residence of President Kennedy, and from the headlines in the paper, the club president's instructions are still appropriate: "Get on our knees and pray." In spite of the fact that our present President's astuteness at politics is unparalleled, somehow we seem more and more inclined to rely on the machinations of man than on the eternal wisdom and plans of God. And the real blunder of it all is that we don't take even a moment to consider how much we've lost "touch." The French lady was right when she said, "Man doesn't meditateth enough."

Tonight, in this city of history, I shall meditate.

It was through his rumination that Walter came to accept the fact that he could only accomplish so much on the home front when he was there so little. So he doubled his efforts to make up ground when he was home—more hunting trips with the boys on the weekends and Major League Baseball games in the evenings; dinner double-dates with Walter's associates and their wives. Lunches at local country clubs with neighbors who were becoming good friends. What made up the most ground on Walter's behalf, however, was Speedy's strength and resolve.

Family meals at home were not frequent so Speedy treated them like holidays, serving premium steaks and a scratch-made pie for dessert. It always made for a memorable event and the family began to look forward to the next "holiday." Then Walter was gone again, her daily bridge group and the regular game nights for neighboring moms and their children kept the house lively and well-traveled. It also helped the boys acclimate through new friendships.

***

On October 5, 1966, Walter presented Speedy with her second album. As she had done the previous year, she received it with gratitude and then allowed the letters to refresh her strength while Walter traveled. Then as their effect began to fade during the cold winter nights, she dug deeper into the Cleveland soil without a single sigh, blank stare, or complaint.

She didn't admit there was an issue weighing on her that she could not identify, nor could many Clevelanders. The city was growing in its instability. Cleveland had fallen into a steady economic decline that would eventually topple it from its pedestal as an American industrial powerhouse. The decline reached every part of the city, including the Berans' upscale neighborhood of Shaker Heights. The Hough Riots in July of 1966 critically injured thirty people and killed four black Americans, including Joyce Arnett, a twenty- six year-old mother of three. The victims were more than a symbol of the nation's racial tensions. They were a local catalyst that compelled city officials to promote a strategy that would eventually implode Cleveland.

In an effort to stop the economic bleeding officials, with the support of key local businesses, focused on protecting and preserving Cleveland's downtown. It didn't work. Cleveland's population steadily declined in the latter half of the decade—especially in urban areas—leaving the local businesses with a thinning customer base and workforce.

She didn't know it yet, but Speedy was sensing the early rumblings of the implosion. It left her feeling unstable. When Walter presented her with his third installment of letters, his words reinvigorated her from October to the New Year. Then something happened that she didn't expect. Their effect didn't wane as they had in years past. Instead, a mathematical effect kicked in with which Walter was very familiar. Compound interest.

The letters' impact on Speedy began catching up to Walter's initial expectations. With each shared experience and vivid recollection, each "Thank you" and "I think of you often!" and "I miss you!" a bulletproof case was being built that was now some 250 letters strong. The evidence was undeniable. It showed that Walter's work was not only *his* work. She was there with him on all his journeys. He had allowed it to be so. More than that, he had invited her in, again and again.

It was a bitter winter night on Lyman Circle and the boys had been asleep for some time when Speedy found herself finally receiving that invitation. A change commenced inside her even while the circumstances around her destabilized. She began to pore back over Walter's letters from 1964 to 1967. She could suddenly see herself sitting next to him on the plane as he reviewed his notes and smiled at her. She could see herself studying his kind eyes and square jaw as he presented a solution to the executives of some major firm in Detroit or Chicago or Dallas...then listening to him order for her at a nice restaurant...and then resting her head on his chest in the hotel bed.

Walter was forty-one and though he was not present to receive it, he was being given his greatest gift on a cold dark night in Cleveland. While he was asleep in a hotel room in Chicago, Speedy caught his vision—that his work was never for the sake of working, that there was no success in succeeding if his success did not impact the lives of others. He'd been saying it time and again in the letters. Now the realization struck a chord in her. She considered her own dreams—for herself, for their boys, for the world.

Speedy flipped back to a letter written in August 1967. She remembered it because Walter had broken protocol. She and the boys were visiting her mother in Poteet and Walter was home alone with their dachshund Miss Maybe. He used the occasion to pen a series of letters that summarized the scope of who he was and who he intended to become. Speedy now placed herself there with him.

August 3, 1967

A thought which keeps running uppermost in my mind is the reply of a father to his teenage son to the question, "Dad, what did you do in World War II?" The reply: "Son, I lived."

That's a rather profound reply. Somehow, when people ask me, "How are you?" my reply is, "I'm alive." And it has profound meaning. Its meaning is very simple, though. It simply means that I have another chance, or a first chance, or some power to act—to will what this very moment will be. In spite of all the failure to move the ball on past downs, I've got another down coming, so to speak. I have but to try. And this makes life the exciting experience it can be.

> *I'm not certain what tomorrow will bring, but if I'm alive, I've got a chance to influence its course for good or bad. I'm ready for tomorrow.*
> *In my calendar there is a note written in at the top of each page, which simply says, "Dive in!" I hope I do.*

When Walter presented Speedy with her next album on October 5, 1968, she devoured it as one would a full report of the last year of her own life. She knew that while the calendar would show they had spent more days apart than together, in a spiritual sense they had never been apart. They had only been doubling their effort, she at home and he abroad. She knew the score at home. John had become a 17-year-old hippie. He was still a source of much prayer, but he hadn't run away again. Jim was still jolly, only jolly on puberty. He seemed to have acquired far more female friends than the average boy his age. Many prayers had been offered there, too. Walter's nightmares hadn't subsided but they had become an accepted part of her life, if they had to be.

What Speedy didn't know was the accumulating score on Walter's watch.

As she poured over his letters spanning from the fall of 1967 to the fall of 1968, the score became clear. Walter's stock in Ernst was rising by the week as he continued raising the bar for himself and the company.

The federal government was seeking to privatize public agencies and one of the first was the U.S. Post Office, who ultimately sought to operate like a private enterprise. An important step in the process was hiring an outside auditor to establish the baseline and clarify opportunities for efficiency and growth. Walter had pounced on the opening. In a matter of two weeks, he secured a meeting. Within two months he had acquired the U.S. Post Office as a client. He then put a team together who would conduct the first ever audit of the federal organization. It was a huge coup for the company, so much so that the Cleveland headquarters created a 3x5-foot cardboard postage stamp of Walter's bust and displayed it in the main hallway. The coup also provided some comic relief in Walter's busy schedule.

After learning no mail had been delivered for nearly three weeks from the Post Office in a rural Texas town, Walter paid the postmaster a personal visit. He was a cheerful, pipe-smoking old man with spectacles.

He greeted Walter with a thick drawl and a firm grip. Walter squeezed his hand and introduced himself as a boy who grew up in The Grove. For a few minutes the two reminisced about days gone by and then Walter let the old man know why he was there.

When he inquired about the missing mail, the old postmaster thumbed over his shoulder to a canvas sack in the corner behind him.

"Bag's not full yet," he explained.

***

While his value in the company had begun to multiply, the days away from home also had a cumulative effect. Speedy found strength in Walter's strength and vulnerability.

> *November 26, 1967*
> *...Time passes so swiftly and there are so many things I get involved in that I want to get accomplished that I rarely pause to be conscious of that which is so near and dear and true — and that includes you. I doubt, though, that the situation will change much, and I trust you'll endure me in spite of it because the very thing which motivates me — you and the boys — I devote the least time to. What a cockeyed paradox. Yet, whenever I move into a challenging situation, my brief prayer is, "Lord, grant that I may be a credit to you, Speedy, the boys, and my firm. Give me challenges, but make me equal to them."*

Three months later, Walter offered Speedy his solution for this challenge of time, written like a true accountant.

> *February 13, 1968*
> *I sometimes wonder whether it wouldn't be a great idea for people to prepare a daily "profits and losses" statement, somewhat like businesses do annually. The idea is to come to the close of each day, such as this one, and answer the question, "Now, what was I for today— what was my reason for being? Was it beneficial to my*

*family, to my firm, to God and country and to society
that I was alive and did the things I did today? Or were
the things I left undone—which were many—injurious
to anyone? Regardless of the consequences, what inac-
tions must I add to my list of indolent activities?*

*I think such a scoreboard would serve a useful pur-
pose because it would goad into action people like
Walter Beran.*

As Walter's responsibilities grew around him, a steadfastness grew
inside him. Through his letters, it grew inside Speedy, too. She attended
Jim's football games and wrestling matches with his friends' mothers.
Afterward, they all descended on the Beran house, which had become
a second home to John and Jim's friends, who called her "Mom B."
One day, Speedy returned home from the grocery store and began preparing for dinner only to find that Jim's lanky friend Rick had placed
all the dishes on the top shelf of the cabinets. Speedy had to retrieve
them while standing on a chair from the dining room.

As the Berans found their footing, it seemed everywhere around
them was deteriorating. By Walter's count, from the September 30, 1962
Ole Miss riot to the August 1968 Democratic National Convention riot
in Chicago, there had been twenty-eight major riots across the nation.

In the midst of the outward turmoil, Walter internalized his efforts.
This included bridging the divide his work schedule had created
between him and his family. Even if the nation would not stabilize,
the Berans would be a unified front—a grove of oaks standing firm in
the storms.

Walter knew John would graduate soon and he worried what step
he would take. A soldier? A college student? Something else? John had
not been raised under the protective watch of an entire community, nor
had he grown up in an environment that required him to be resourceful.
Now he was nearly the same age at which his father had shipped off
to fight a war, and yet Walter could not imagine his son taking on such
a responsibility—especially if that war were in the tangled jungles of
Vietnam. Walter worried that he had not prepared John well enough to
know which wars were worth fighting.

He worried less about Jim, who still seemed content to chase girls
and help his mother while his dad was away. There would need to be a

conversation at some point on the former topic, but Jim was not there yet. The conversation Walter did bring up concerned a different sort of desire in Jim. "What are you going to do with your life?" Walter would ask him.

"I don't know yet," was Jim's response. Walter continued to prod.

John's answer wasn't so simple. He was already a reflection of the forces in conflict across the nation. He was struggling to find his place amidst them.

Then at 6:01 PM on April 4, 1968, a gunshot took the life of Martin Luther King, Jr. while he stood on the second-story balcony of the Lorraine Hotel in Memphis, Tennessee. John was a junior in high school and the following days at school shook him as he observed peers who were indifferent, almost irreverent, and peers who'd been traumatized. He was sickened that there was even a divide. A man whom his father and many others respected, a man who had not harmed another soul, was killed in cold blood.

John had been alive when the President Kennedy was assassinated, but he was five years younger and it did not get to him as this did. Suddenly, he struggled to make sense of waking up in a place where something like this could happen. He wanted out. More precisely, he wanted to go home. There was more in Texas than John was saying. Two years before the family moved to Cleveland, he met a girl in Poteet on a hay ride and fell in love with her.

The evening after Walter returned from a trip to Detroit, 16-year-old John informed his father of his plans to leave for Texas the next day — to hell with Cleveland. Walter led John into the back room and this time he did not withhold his emotions. Neither did John. A shouting match eventually erupted that reached every corner of the house. When Jim heard the commotion he ran up the stairs to find Walter and John in a shoving match. Jim pushed John away and screamed, "What the hell is wrong with you?" It killed the momentum of the fight. Walter asked Jim to step out of the room. A succinct offer was made.

If John wanted to go to Texas, he could. It would just be on his father's terms. He would attend a military academy. John agreed to the terms and three months later, Walter dropped his son off at the Texas Military Institute in San Antonio where he would finish out his final two years of high school. Walter hoped it was the right play.

A few days after the fight, Jim asked his dad an unexpected question. "Why do you never swear?" He had noticed that even in the midst of a heated exchange that nearly came to blows, Walter managed to keep his cool and hold his tongue.

Walter told Jim a story from The Grove. When he was a young boy at school one day, he called another boy a son of a bitch. He was immediately sent to the school minister, where he prepared for a physical and verbal lashing. Instead, the minister sat him down and gently explained how every person is created in the image of God and therefore every person is glorious.

"I've never forgotten that lesson," concluded Walter.

Jim nodded.

Speedy at home in the Cleveland snow.

Walter & Speedy E&E Party 1966

7

Reckoning

Walter was shaken by the assassination of Martin Luther King, Jr. and he saw much of his teenaged self in young John's response. Now that he was older and more discerning, the events surrounding them were not all that surprising. "Maybe we've gone our way long enough," he wrote to Speedy a few days after the tragedy. "Maybe the age old truths are still man's best guide for behavior."

The death of Martin Luther King, Jr. did not impact Walter as it did John, but it was no less a force that helped him finally put words to all he'd been experiencing, including John's struggles.

> *May 8, 1968*
>
> *...We don't have roots anymore. Our society hasn't any and neither do its individual constituents. Mobility, the rapid pace of things, change, planned obsolescence, the "God is dead" theory, lessening of property rights— all these tear at the roots. And, I suppose, mobility has had as great an impact as anything. Maybe I sense this because I'm a participant in it.*
>
> *There isn't any question that our move to Cleveland has expanded our exposure, our horizons have broadened, there's a thrill in what I do, we've come to know new faces and met many wonderful people; yet, it's doubtful that we've made many, if any, real friends, like the ones who are the bedrock kind back in San*

Antonio. Friendship takes a lot of mixing in life's cru-
cible. Most drop out along the way. The true ones settle
to the bottom after a lot of stirring. And this kind of root
structure is lost when mobility takes place.

Another kind of root structure is lost, too. It's the
commonality of what you and others believe in alike.
Unless you've worked with others for some time, moti-
vated by the same issues of faith, the pleasantries of
the day which are exchanged are lacking in genuine
rapport. Mobility tears at the heart of this; it decimates
the sense of oneness; it erodes away a foundation built
by working alongside and with others, elbow to elbow!

Identity is lost in mobility. I suspect my share of
observation on this. Although I have significant iden-
tity in the firm, I sometimes feel it's more bestowed than
real in spite of the fact I hope I'm measuring up and
exceeding expectations. In San Antonio we plowed our
path to community identification.

So it's not difficult to understand society's confusion;
why young boys like John David defy the order of things.

Walter's clarity did more than name society's core issue. It also
validated Speedy's vulnerabilities in Cleveland. Ohio was not Texas.
Despite a genuine investment into the lives and times of Lyman Circle,
despite bridge buddies, memorable dinners at the club, and meaningful
friendships that would stand the test of time, Cleveland simply did not
feel like home. The one question that remained was what Cleveland
would come to mean.

The answer was becoming clearer to Walter and he hoped he was
transferring that clarity to Speedy. As he saw it, their lack of roots in
Cleveland urged him to consider the larger community his work created.

While there were practical tasks to be done—audits, projections, rec-
ommendations—as a twenty-year veteran, that work had become routine. Walter knew he could do it well. His standards would not change.

The rising standard was in how he could protect, lift, and serve those
whose paths he crossed every day, not merely through his accounting
practice but also through his accountability to the debt he owed a world
that had saved him. The Grove had protected him when he could not

protect himself. Its people had lifted him when he could barely walk, and they had served him selflessly for seventeen years. The same was also true of those French fishermen whose faces he never knew, the old French woman in the lonely café and, of course, Speedy. His work provided the greatest opportunity to repay his debt. To meet the challenge, he would need Speedy more than ever.

> *June 8, 1969*
>
> *The press of this tight traveling schedule leaves little time for contemplation, time to meditate, time to think ahead and let the mind wander for ideas. I recall the French lady (and a lady in her 70s she was)...she kept telling me that the American male never put the brakes on—to stop, to pause, to muse, to contemplate, to let the mind wander wherever it wished to take him. She coaxed me to be different—to stroll through the garden (as if I had one) at day's end and at break of dawn to commune with nature, to absorb the quiet beauty of God's creation and capture the freshness of ideas to see through the maze of complexity of the day with the clear eyes of nature, to regain perspective and remove oneself for a moment, at least, from the rat-race which is the syndrome in which the American male lives.*
>
> *She must have been right, my dear and wonderful French lady of years ago and miles away. Certainly, she must have gone on to her reward, yet her advice continues to ring clear.*

On March 12, 1970, Walter wrote to Speedy about the bombings of three major buildings in New York City, including a location where two associates kept offices. The destruction would soon be linked to the organization known as the Weather Underground, a radical left group characterized by Black power, anti-imperialism, and violent opposition to the Vietnam War. The group's ultimate goal was to create a revolutionary party that would eventually overthrow the U.S. government, which they considered a threat to democracy.

As Walter pointed out, the latest acts of violence were additional signs of an imminent collapse and the more he traveled the more obvious the collapse became. By this time Walter's perspective was changing. Within the larger community of his work, he had found a consistent reason for hope in the world's future, ironically from the same generation that had spawned Weather Underground. After speaking to a group of students at Emory University in Atlanta, he wrote to Speedy the following:

> *March 12, 1970*
>
> *When you read this, you will remember that this was a time when bombings were rampant in New York City. Last night three major downtown buildings were bombed...*
>
> *Yet, there is hope. When a group of college students stands up for what an "old man" says—as they did in Atlanta the other night — there is hope and good reason for a lot of it, and it's simply because there are a lot of youngsters (most as a matter of fact) like the Emory group, who have a good sense of what is right and true.*

Walter never wrote specifically about where he stood on the Vietnam War or on the waves of local and national protests. However, as these continued unresolved, he increasingly pointed Speedy to his faith in the "fine young students" of America. It was these same students who would just a few weeks later become a tragic symbol of both the growing U.S. sentiment on the war and, ironically, of hope.

On April 30, 1970, President Nixon issued his Cambodia Incursion address to the nation. The U.S. would invade Cambodia, further escalating a war that fewer and fewer understood. Protests mounted, especially on university and college campuses like those at Kent State, where six days later the Ohio National Guard fired off sixty-seven rounds of ammunition into a loose crowd of protestors and passersby, ending the lives of four students and permanently paralyzing a fifth from the chest down. A week later, an estimated 4,000,000 fellow students at universities, colleges, and high schools across the country held a strike that forced hundreds of their institutions to temporarily close.

In response, Walter held tighter to Speedy and their own students, John and Jim, who were now in college and high school, respectively. Both had become young men who, Walter insisted, made his "heart proud as a father." Yet he still worried how they were processing the events unfolding around them.

Jim was still living at home and attending high school. While he was certainly not sheltered from the national melee, he was easier to summarize: sports, food, and girls. He was less motivated than Walter had hoped, evidenced by his inability to answer his father's frequent inquiries about what he wanted to do with his life. Jim wasn't shy about his answer. He didn't have one. He did, however, have a plaque.

That summer Jim attended a local renaissance fair and purchased a marble desk plaque with an engraving that read: "All things come to he that waiteth." Once home, he promptly placed it on the desk in his father's home office. Surely that would get him off his back.

Two weeks later, Jim returned to the home office looking for a paperclip and noticed his marble plaque was gone. In its place was a wooden desk plaque Walter had commissioned a local artisan to make. It read: "All things come to he that waiteth as long as while he waiteth he worketh like hell."

If that didn't motivate Jim, one incident permanently changed his opinion of his father's advice. He'd awoken one night when he heard screams coming from his parents' room. He jumped out of bed and ran to the room thinking it was his mom in distress only to discover his dad on the floor in a fetal position, sweating profusely and still in a state of sleep. Jim shook Speedy awake and together they helped Walter out of the nightmare and back into bed.

When Jim asked his dad what the nightmare was about, Walter said, "I was trapped in a fox hole." The experience made it difficult for Jim to be unclear about the foolishness of his own inertia.

John had received a student deferment from the war and was studying at the University of Texas in Austin, a 40,000-student epicenter of political activism and experimentation. Students there had already led a 25,000-person march in response to the Kent State shootings. Walter didn't know where John stood. He only hoped he was standing firm in what mattered most.

Walter leaned toward hope despite his parental concerns. He was nearing fifty and it was becoming easier to reflect on a "much younger" time when he had not been so certain of himself or where he was heading. While on a plane heading southwest, he thought back on his days in The Grove when he'd easily get lost in the woods. At one point it had become so frequent that no one — not an adult, not his brothers, not even Lawrence — would let him wander freely on a possum hunt because they'd inevitably have to abandon the hunt and go in search of him.

He then thought of another similar incident that took place when he was John's age—eighteen years old—and his infantry unit was in combat training. He was designated the lead scout and charged with guiding his battalion through the woods to address a "problem," as the officer had termed it. Walter led them so far off track that instead of confronting the problem they discovered the Red Cross coffee and doughnut truck, from which all partook. Walter was never asked to lead a battalion again.

Walter worried that his boys would get lost too, but not merely on a possum hunt or a training exercise in a benign forest.

A week later on a cab ride in Manhattan, Walter told Speedy that he was "pleasantly reminded that despite the poor choices people make or the mistaken paths they take, most are quite resilient...," just as he had been. Walter described the cabbie as an older man in his sixties "who'd been hacking around for forty-one years." He had only one eye. The other had been lost when he was attacked with a cast iron rod and robbed. "Yet," Walter marveled, "he was cheerful and had a considerate and concerned attitude...a human oasis in New York City."

In a letter to Speedy that followed, Walter explained how the seemingly mundane experience "reinforced the fact that there are still a lot of good people around."

It was the same experience that got Walter thinking about the importance of what he called "small steps," a nod to the Apollo 11 mission he and the world had just witnessed a few months earlier. These small steps were as simple as the cheerful attitude of the cabbie in New York or a half-page letter to Speedy while away or a practice he subsequently began on every one of his flights.

At the time, scientists couldn't explain how bumblebees flew because their wings were too small for their mass. Walter loved its meaning because it symbolized a person's ability to accomplish the impossible. He would wave a flight attendant over and say, "You've heard about the bumblebee, right? Scientist say that it shouldn't be able to fly because its wings are two small for its mass, but here it comes." With that he stuck the bumblebee on her lapel as he explained its significance.

Thirty years later, Jim was on a flight and noticed an old worn out bumblebee on the name tag of a flight attendant. He asked her where she got it and she said, "From the nicest man I ever met, many years ago."

Jim asked if he was "a short guy with graying hair."

The attendant chimed back, "Why, yes!"

Jim then replied, "I've met that guy—he's a jerk," to which the woman immediately took issue. She laced into him until Jim confessed he was joking and the man was actually his dad. He received excellent service for the remainder of the flight.

Soon the bumblebees were replaced by embroidered roses. Alone, each was an act that might soon be forgotten—a small step with little progress — but cumulatively the small steps would build to a "giant leap for mankind" or a "sum of goodness" if they were pointed in the same direction.

> *October 6, 1970*
>
> *This note begins a new series. The fact that it is a new series certainly holds no promises of a lot of new in the series. I suspect you and the girls who have to decipher these notes will be subject to a lot of the same. And that seems to be typical of life—a lot of the sameness…. The challenge is to make the sameness good and positive, and moving toward a desirable goal….*
>
> *Today several of us from E&E flew down on the same flight. The red roses created a real rapport with the stewardesses and a lady who said she was 84. She got a rose, too. Upon leaving the plane in Miami, she grabbed my arms and said, "I like you, you have a happy soul." I hope that holds true forever, and ever, and ever and ever….*

Two weeks later, instead of embroidered roses, Walter began handing out smile buttons. They were as much to foster his optimistic perspective as to bolster others'. By late spring 1971, Walter was handing out embroidered hearts when he rode on a Boeing 747 for the first time. It was symbolic of the heights to which his career had taken him and he enjoyed a glass of wine in-flight to celebrate the occasion, leaving the last swallow for the old French lady. A few days later, while waiting for a flight from Cleveland to Milwaukee, Walter took note of a man "who looked like a ghost" as two friends assisted him into the airport bathroom. Once in flight, the man once again had to be assisted to the plane's bathroom. Moments later a request came over the public address system for a doctor. There was no answer.

For the remainder of the flight, the lifeless body of the man lie in the aisle at the forward entrance covered with airline blankets.

Walter felt the timing was unmistakable. He confessed to Speedy that it was a reminder of how fragile success is, and how the wisest people learn to number their days and make the most of every opportunity.

Three months later, the vice chairman and managing partner of Ernst's Western region passed away suddenly. Walter was promoted to replace him. It meant a monumental raise. It also meant another move—to Los Angeles.

Letters to Speedy

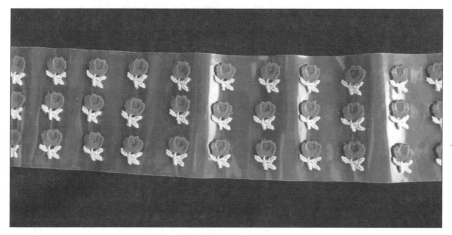

Handing out Roses

8

Redemption

W hen Walter accepted, the new position with Ernst in early fall 1971, the Cleveland office hired two people to replace him. Meanwhile, Walter wasted no time finding a new home in their new city. In a letter to Speedy, he called the bank crazy for loaning them $250,000 for the house. He was no less grateful. "It's a great house with a fantastic view," he wrote, and then concluded, "God is mysterious, but especially good to me."

A month later, Jim graduated from high school. The next night he and three friends jumped in his yellow Buick and headed west where they would eventually meet up with his parents at their new address: 600 Clinton Place, Beverly Hills, CA 90210. When Speedy first laid eyes on the huge house she exclaimed, "We've been redeemed!"

Their home sat midway up a tiered neighborhood called Trousdale Estates, which was built in the 1950s and 60s on what used to be Doheny Ranch. Nestled in the hills above Sunset Boulevard, the homes faced west-southwest so that on a clear day you could see Port of Long Beach and Catalina Island in the distance.

After all their belongings had finally been transported to new drawers, closets and cabinets and the furniture had been arranged, Walter penned a quick letter, which he recounted to Speedy in person the following day.

June 11, 1972

When I think of the last several days and nights, I'm convinced more than ever that I'm going to write a book someday on roots. At the moment you are in Texas, where our real roots were once. But many of them have eroded...and somewhere in between, John and Jim have never been still long enough to have anchored many roots anywhere. John, of course, is probably getting his planted pretty good, yet those Jim has for the most part were pulled up with his graduation Thursday night.

But it's time to plant some more. We must and we will. And we'll find other new friends to add to those beautiful ones already on our list. And we'll experience new discoveries. And we'll find new reasons to add to our faith. And we'll learn that our love will take on added dimensions of strength, understanding, and the joy of each other's presence.

By the time Speedy recounted the actual letter within the pages of her next birthday album—October 1971 to October 1972—their roots had already begun to grow. They had met and befriended several neighbors who together formed a unique community held together by mutual privacy and prominence. Record executive Mike Curb, who produced Sammy Davis, Jr.'s "Candy Man," Debby Boone's "You Light Up My Life" and numerous songs by Donny and Marie, lived just below them. Speedy babysat his children. The country's last Five-Star General, Omar Bradley, lived three houses away. Walter hoped Jim might learn a thing or two from the iconic leader. He hoped the same for himself. Around the corner lived Dean Martin, whose speeding Stutz Bearcat had run Jim's Buick off a neighborhood street that summer. Budding tennis great Jimmy Connors lived a few doors down and liked to jog in the middle of the streets. Jim nearly learned this tidbit the hard way. He was leaving the neighborhood one day and narrowly missed running the lefty over. Jim turned to flip him off and then saw his face. His one-fingered fist morphed into a wave. Other neighbors included Wide World of Sports creator Andy Sedaris, comic pioneers Carol Burnett and Phyllis Diller, singer-songwriter Kenny Rogers, preeminent jockey Willie Shoemaker, and 50s pop icon Pat Boone.

It was quite an adjustment moving to Clinton Place from Lyman Circle, let alone via The Grove and Poteet. Still, the opportunities for friendship excited Speedy not because these were famous people, but for a more practical reason. There was always someone around during the day. With the boys gone, she would have the chance to foster her community in a way she hadn't since college.

The friendships excited Walter, too. He'd felt the lack of roots in Cleveland much more than Speedy. Being so transient, there was little opportunity for him to savor the stability of tradition and familiarity. Outside the constancy of his marriage and paycheck, all else was nomadic. Walter believed Los Angeles would be their home for good. God willing, it would be where he'd retire one day and finally get to read from his growing collection of books and partake from his swelling stockpile of fine wine. It would also be the city where his work would be most remembered.

There was another element of their new home that excited him. It was something he kept to himself at first. He let it marinate: In their neighborhood alone, they were surrounded by people with great means, people of great accomplishment and influence. Walter knew that if such people rallied together, they could make a big impact. He tucked away the thought and went about his duties at Ernst.

What Walter didn't yet see was that his vision to grow roots and make a lasting impact in Los Angeles would be challenged by the troubled soul of the city. Los Angeles, in 1972, was disproportionately controlled by the "WASP" elite—White, Anglo-Saxon Protestants with status and privilege who stood atop the food chain in the business community, education circles, and city government. While the WASP enclave had been prominent in major U.S. cities since before World War II — and while the money and business prowess of its members was a major reason L.A. was the third and soon-to-be second largest city in America — their unspoken status quo (whether or not it was deliberate) had created a citywide infrastructure that was fractured along jagged religious and racial lines.

Still lingering was the tension and socioeconomic divide personified on August 11, 1965, when a 21-year-old black American young man named Marquette Frye was pulled over by white California Highway Patrol motorcycle officer Lee Minikus on suspicion of drunk driving. Minikus immediately radioed for backup. Frye's mother, Rena

Price, lived nearby and quickly arrived on the scene to scold her son. According to Frye, someone then shoved his mother and a skirmish ensued that ended with Frye, Price, and Frye's brother being arrested at the end of a police shotgun.

By then, crowds had gathered and the tension had escalated. Rocks and pieces of concrete flew from the crowd at the policemen and their vehicles. The Frye brothers and their mother were quickly removed from the area in police cruisers, but the acrimony had already reached a tipping point.

Six days of violent clashes ensued between Watts residents and both local and national law enforcement. This included outbreaks of looting, severe property damage, and attacks on white business owners and motorists. When the riots finally ended on the 17th of April, 34 people were dead, another 3,438 were arrested, and over 1,000 buildings were disfigured or destroyed to the tune of $40 million in property damage.

Seven years had passed by the time Walter and Speedy arrived, but the underlying tension still existed. When mixed with rising national unemployment and inflation, it made for a cracking foundation that was largely ignored by the wealthy members of the city's premier private clubs: the Los Angeles Country Club, the California Club, and the Jonathan Club, all of which Walter would become a member.

While no club would acknowledge published bylaws that prohibited members of other races, religions or genders, the unofficial nod was that only white men were welcome through their doors with the occasional exception for prominent families outside that sphere. The result was that the city's premier watering holes functioned more like symbols of the city's dangerous divide.

The irony is that one of the city's rising leaders was a man by the name of Tom Bradley, the grandson of a slave. Bradley was born to poor sharecroppers in a small log cabin on the outskirts of Calvert, Texas, a mid-sized town of 2,500 people, only eighty miles southeast of The Grove. In 1924, when he was seven years old, the Bradley family, including Tom's four siblings, moved to the Temple-Alvarado section of Los Angeles where his father became a railroad porter and his mother a maid.

Bradley rose from his humble beginnings the moment he was afforded an opportunity. At Polytechnic High School, he became the first black to be elected president of the Boys League and the first to be inducted into the Ephebians national honor society. Bradley also excelled as an athlete and in 1937 began attending UCLA on an athletic scholarship. In 1940, he joined the Los Angeles Police Department, becoming one of only 400 black men to serve on the force of more than 4,000 officers. Bradley retired from the LAPD as a police lieutenant after twenty-three years and after completing law school during his final years on the force. In 1963, he became the first black to be elected to the Los Angeles City Council, winning the 10th District seat over the incumbent Joe Hollingsworth. Bradley's intention as a city councilman was clear from the beginning. He once explained to a *Los Angeles Times* reporter that his time and energy were best spent bringing the diverse groups of the city together.

Remaining true to his word, Bradley worked tirelessly to bridge the fractured community infrastructure that was knowingly and unknowingly being fostered by the city's elite. In hopes of making a greater and more direct impact, he ran for Los Angeles Mayor in 1969 against incumbent Mayor Sam Yorty, a fellow Democrat. With support from several prominent city leaders, Bradley held a substantial lead in the primary but was forced into a runoff with Yorty who promptly played the racial card, citing fears that as Mayor, Bradley would allow Black Nationalists a stake in the city's future. Yorty came from behind in the polls and handed Bradley a shocking defeat. Tom Bradley was not deterred.

By the time Walter and Speedy had finally settled into their new home in Beverly Hills in the fall of 1972, Bradley was on the campaign trail a second time seeking to unseat Sam Yorty in the 1973 mayoral election. Walter was taking in the upcoming election as any newcomer to the city would but, without a taste for politics, he remained an outside observer whose primary curiosity was which of the two Democrats was best for business growth. Los Angeles had played second fiddle to New York long enough where trade with the Far East was concerned, and Walter viewed changing this as an integral part of the Ernst's growth — and the future of Los Angeles. In Walter's worldview, there were more important things than political rhetoric. He was more interested in finding key allies who shared his philosophy of business and who would help him expand his impact.

***

For their first Christmas in L.A., Walter and Speedy planned a holiday dinner with three other couples at a small Italian restaurant called L'Estrada. The boys were both on break from college, John from Texas and Jim from UCLA, and they'd been shooed off to their own holiday endeavors that night. Walter and Speedy relished an evening with locals whom they hoped would become dear friends. Their conversations flowed freely as did their drinks, and three hours had passed by the time the couples finally stood and made their way to the valet stand. Also waiting for her car was German sex symbol Elke Sommer, one of the top movie actresses of the 1960s and 70s. When her vehicle arrived, she began kissing her friends goodbye. Seeing this, Walter strolled over to Sommer and said, "What about me?"

She looked down at him from her high heels somewhat confused. Then she chimed, "But of course!" and laid a big kiss on Walter's lips. Then, turning to Speedy, Walter beamed, "don't I get one from you too?" Speedy couldn't resist, shaking her head and laughing "But of course!" After getting the kiss from Speedy Walter exclaimed " God, it's great to be in Los Angeles!"

***

A few weeks later, Walter was back on the road when life prodded him again. As his plane landed late in Spokane, a shooting was taking place at his gate. He deplaned shortly after the body had been removed. There were still pools of blood. He could not shake the sight as he rode the cab to his hotel. It was yet another reminder of the fragility of life.

He was nearing his final decade with Ernst. There was a good case for coasting. He'd arrived in Trousdale Estates and the boys had survived their teens and seemed to be building good lives of their own, but what purpose would that serve other than his own?

In the middle of that same night in Spokane, Walter shot up in his bed drenched in sweat and shivering again. Calmly, he rose from the bed and walked to the bathroom. He splashed his face with two handfuls of water and dabbed his face with a towel. Then he changed his shirt and climbed back into bed. Instead of falling asleep, he wrote Speedy with a vulnerable request.

March 14, 1973

Speedy, keep inspiring; keep understanding, patiently. Keep bringing me back to the simple equations. Keep me getting excited over possibility, over how to get others excited.

Perhaps, all I need is you and the possibility of a spot—some day—in Texas, or California, or...to do nothing but spend time with you.

P.S. To spend time with you is not nothing. It's everything.

No one would blame Walter if he was feeling a little burned out. Yet that letter to Speedy was the closest he ever came to admitting he was weary. As his days played out they proved weariness to be a fleeting feeling, or at least an easy one to hide. Whenever weariness crept in, he quickly thought of The Grove and the Dubes and Rosie Symm and the old French lady. They'd given him something greater than his birthright; they'd give him opportunity and the will to be great. A grateful man doesn't need more than that. His unfit heart had outlived its prognosis. Now he was living in the third largest city in America and working from a prominent corporate position. Was it all just coincidence? Walter was convinced it wasn't.

In the weeks that followed, Walter pondered how to expand his efforts. Soon, a plan came into focus. As the summer of 1973 approached, Walter sought a teammate who would share his vision and know how to help him activate it. However, there was a problem. She was already employed as an executive with California Federal Bank. Her name was Marrgo "with two r's" Rosato, an attractive, fit brunette who in heels stood eye-to-eye with Walter.

He met Marrgo at an event in April put on by an executive women's organization that Ernst supported. Walter was not easily impressed, but Marrgo's presence made an immediate impact. When she shook Walter's hand, her grip was so firm it surprised him and he said so. The same sense of strength came through when she spoke. Walter could not forget her. As far as he was concerned, the search was over. He tracked down Marrgo's number and invited her to lunch at the California Club. There he cast the vision for his daily work and the impact he hoped to make. Walter then offered Marrgo twice what she was earning to serve as his executive assistant. She asked for a few days to consider and during that time the California Federal Bank promised to make her an officer if she stayed. It wasn't enough. Marrgo was equally impressed with Walter. She officially became his right hand on August 15, 1973.

Two weeks later, Walter walked into her office and heaved a three-inch binder on her desk.

"What is it?" Marrgo asked.

"It's the list of all the people I know," Walter replied. Her task was to make sure Walter remained in regular contact with all of them, according to priority and including timely gifts, congratulations, and condolences.

Marrgo promptly convinced Walter to let her hire an assistant to compile all the information into a database where it could easily be accessed and utilized. Three weeks later, the job was finished and a system of regular calls, cards, and shared meals was underway. Walter was impressed. Then he handed Marrgo another binder, smaller than the first.

"What is it?" Marrgo asked again.

"It's the list of all the people I *want* to know," Walter replied.

For the occasion, Walter asked Marrgo to shrink and laminate dozens of business card-sized copies of a cartoon by Jim Berry. On it is a sketch of a balding businessman with glasses sitting on one end of a couch at a party. He is waving to the well-to-do woman sitting at the other end of the couch. The caption reads: "Hi, I'm one of the very few remaining Walters."

The second list of names would become Marrgo's focus for the next decade. Trips to the copy store for more laminated cartoons became routine as did scheduling regular contact with each person according to the nature of the budding relationship—a monthly meal with those who were local, a monthly letter to friends and associates outside L.A., and formal meetings as needed with those whom Walter was representing, managing, mentoring, or wanting to know better.

There were also the appropriate celebratory gifts for each person throughout the year and sympathy notes for those who'd lost loved ones. For the latter, Walter had Marrgo shrink, copy, and laminate several dozen business card sized copies of an unknown quote he felt described personal loss beautifully. It read:

I am standing up on the seashore. A ship at my side spreads her white sails to the morning breeze and starts for the blue ocean. I stand and watch her until at length she hangs like a speck of white cloud just where the sea and sky come down to mingle with each other. Then someone at my side says: "There! She's Gone."

Gone where? Gone from my sight—that is all. She is just as large in mast and hull and spar as she was when she left my side. Her diminished size is in me, not in her; just at the moment when someone at my side says, "There! She's gone," there are other eyes watching her coming, and other voices ready to take up the glad shout, "There she Comes!" And that is dying.

The names on the second list were many you would expect a managing partner of a large accounting firm to want to know: executives of companies based in the region who were not yet clients, decision-makers at other accounting and investment firms, and mortgage and banking presidents.

There were also names you would not expect: the governor of California, congressmen and congresswomen in the Western region, pastors of local churches, school administrators, and leaders of local charities. Also on the list were the names of several prominent Japanese businessmen overseas. Walter had done his homework and he saw what he believed to be another potential foundation beneath Los Angeles, and all of southern California for that matter. To that point, the U.S. had only limited trade ties to the Far East and in particular the Pacific Rim, and those that existed were predominately based in Manhattan. It didn't make much logistical sense. The effort didn't accurately reflect the growing need to create more business particularly in Western U.S.

Also on the list was the newly elected Mayor Tom Bradley, who in his second attempt six months earlier had successfully unseated Sam Yorty. It was an historic day for the city as Bradley became the first black Mayor of Los Angeles. It was also fortuitous timing. Tom Bradley and Walter Beran were now influential leaders in the same city. It was only a matter of time before their paths would cross.

On the surface, the two men had nothing in common. Bradley was a tall, black Democrat. Walter was a short, white Republican. Their differences dissolved beneath the surface. Both had grown up dirt poor in small Texas towns picking cotton as small boys. Both had overcome economic disadvantages to become highly successful in their respective fields. Both held to the same philosophy about the role of business in American society.

Tom Bradley faced the same opposition as Walter, but from a different vantage point. Bradley was as an outsider to the influential circle of the WASP elite. He wasn't welcome in their prominent country clubs. However, he now held an advantage. His sat in one of the most powerful positions in a city in which he'd lived and served his entire adult life. He had a credible voice others would have to listen to, even if he didn't fit the bill.

Walter, on the other hand, was becoming an insider. He was, practically speaking, an involuntary member of the city's elite. He was welcomed into the prominent country clubs without knowing what he was stepping into. The ignorance was an advantage.

Walter hadn't been there during the 1940s when Bradley and his new bride Ethel were forced to use a white intermediary to purchase their first home. Walter hadn't lived in Los Angeles in the two decades that followed when Tom Bradley, a member of the Los Angeles Police Department, was not permitted to work with a white officer in the field. Walter wasn't a resident when the Watts Riots took the lives of nearly three dozen people and decimated the city's south side. While Walter was welcomed inside the city's white circle of influence, his lack of history there allowed him to form an objective view of the city's soul where a thick residue of prejudice belied a prosperous, growing city.

***

Walter couldn't articulate it perfectly yet, but he was forming a working philosophy of the role of business—and businesspeople—in society at large. He did not feel it was solely the government's job to fix the ills of society. He felt the job also belonged to the locals, the people with feet on the street who benefitted the most from a thriving economy—in particular, the businesspeople who had the means to create jobs, to sponsor recovery and revitalization wherever it was needed, and to serve and care for their communities. Walter viewed his own daily work as a microcosm of the philosophy in play. Unbeknownst to him, so did the city's mayor.

As Marrgo was checking off the names on Walter's list, Bradley was finalizing the details of a citywide redevelopment plan that included placing influential business leaders on important city committees and spurring major commercial development in the Bunker Hill financial district. While Walter sought the keys to greater impact in the city, Mayor Bradley opened the doors for business leaders just like him to have a tangible say in the future of Los Angeles. The mayor hadn't yet imagined these leaders would include Japanese businessmen.

Walter saw a great opportunity in working with Japan; for Ernst, for Los Angeles, and for the U.S. His inclination to get to know the Japanese businessmen was as much a practical conclusion as business instinct. He believed moving his company's Pacific Rim accounts — some of which had branches in Hawaii — under his management in the West was both logical and responsible. He also felt a greater presence of Japanese businesses could further spark the Los Angeles economy, from which Ernst and every other member of the local community would benefit.

While Walter pushed through his recommendation to move Ernst's Japanese business under his control, Marrgo began planning the local introductions and meetings, which at Walter's request were to be lunches on his dime at one of the three elite clubs. As a member of all three, Walter saw no issues with taking any guest of his choosing through their doors. It wasn't until Marrgo reached out to Mayor Bradley's office with an invitation to lunch with Walter at the California Club that Walter began to see the underbelly of his new home.

The mayor's office thanked Marrgo for the invitation, but respectfully declined. When Marrgo asked for a reason to report back to Water, she was told that Major Bradley did not feel welcome there, with or without a member.

Downtown Los Angeles 1972 Walter's Office View

Redemption in Los Angeles, Marina del Rey 1972

9

Deeper

In the southern California climate, Walter was able to reestablish his old San Antonio habit of taking an early morning jog five days a week. His runs always followed the other daily habit he'd kept since his first year of marriage.

Walter rose at 4:00 AM and began each day by reading from his Luther Bible, a High German language translation, which so often inspired his specific prayers that followed—for every member of his family by name and then for the specific endeavors and challenges before him. This was the deep, spiritual man few people knew except indirectly through the effect he had on them. While Walter was not shy to discuss his faith, which was the axis of his worldview, he never lorded his beliefs about God over another person.

It was his conviction that his faith must be lived out if it was real in the first place and, in the second place, if it was to be of any use to God in the lives of others. The famous passage from Jesus' brother James was a favorite: "For as the body without the spirit is dead, so faith without works is dead also."

So Walter worked not as one trying to accomplish something, but rather as one trying to be as faithful as possible with the life he'd been given. As he saw it, God was keeping him alive for a reason, regardless of what the doctors had said about his weak heart. God would keep him alive as long as he was faithful and there was work for him to do.

In Los Angeles, Speedy was finally free to become a major ally, thanks in part to an offer Walter made to a fellow dad he met at a regional Lutheran Church event in St. Louis during the summer of 1973. Walter had never met the man before, but they happened to sit next to one another during the meal and afterward they struck up a conversation that eventually landed on their children. Walter mentioned Jim and John and their college adventures and the man mentioned his daughter, Jan, who had aspirations of becoming an actress and planned to move to Los Angeles as soon as she was able.

Walter immediately insisted she live with him and Speedy in Beverly Hills until she got settled. It wasn't until he met Jan Burmeister when she arrived at their home in October 1973 that Walter realized he and Speedy were the real benefactors.

Jan was a feisty, blonde-haired, blue-eyed bombshell in her mid-twenties who could have been his and Speedy's own child in that she seemed to possess the outstanding traits of both in one body. She was a natural conversationalist who loved poetry and for whom resourcefulness came easily. Nevertheless, the heritage broke down when it came to height. She stood at least four inches taller than Walter and with heels even taller. Next to Speedy, she looked like Kareem Abdul Jabbar. It was easy to see why she thought she'd have a shot in Hollywood. What the Berans valued most was that Jan was the daughter Speedy had always wanted and she would be around longer than originally planned, which was just fine.

By the time Marrgo was working through Walter's second list of names, Jan had decided to stop pursuing an acting career. Walter snatched her up and made her the official right hand of both Marrgo and Speedy.

The three-pronged attack of Marrgo, Speedy, and Jan became a formidable force and helped build tangible momentum in front of Walter's vision. Through their untiring efforts to connect Walter to the city's influencers and cultivate relationships with Trousdale neighbors and the wives of Walter's clients, Walter was becoming a man to know in L.A. The strategy was quite simple.

Southern California allowed Walter to play host twelve months of the year at some of the best restaurants, events and locales in the country. It was not uncommon for Walter's calendar to be, as a journalist would later describe, more crowded than Malibu beaches on Labor Day, and most of the crowding was self-inflicted. Walter never ate alone. He began every morning with a breakfast meeting in a downtown cafe. Every lunch was spent with another associate or new acquaintance and often more than one, and nearly every dinner was spent entertaining local connections or hosting out of town guests, like a Japanese trade group. After two or three years of this, there was not a good restaurant Walter had not tried—although he had his favorites. Looking back on his life a decade later, a writer for *Westways* magazine asked him to describe his hobbies. Walter looked puzzled. Then he smiled and replied, "I'm going to be a hobby man when I retire."

For Walter's relentless part, his Western region was expanding so rapidly that an old nickname was reborn. Shortly after Walter had accepted his new position in the Cleveland office, the Ernst chairman pulled him aside and, gripping his shoulder, proclaimed, "Beran, you're my eagle!" The moniker stuck and he henceforth referred to Walter as "the eagle." Now the L.A. office had rekindled the flame.

Walter's relational mastery was not complex. He was simply great at being the type of person with whom people wanted to be associated. This was no act—and that made a huge difference. Walter made people feel good. He smiled first and acknowledged his own shortcomings. Then he put people at ease by placing their needs above his own and reinforcing the fact that their best interests were what interested him most. Marrgo's efforts helped him remember the smallest details about each person he contacted. He never missed a birthday (including spouses and children), or an anniversary, or a promotion, or a death in the family. He was also a thoughtful gift-giver, if not a clever one.

On one occasion he sent eight sleeves of golf balls (24 balls in total) to an associate with whom he had recently played a particularly wayward 18-hole round. The associate had received more than one laminated Hope Open card from Walter during the course of play. In fact, Walter gave the man so many he ran out. Of course, Walter was not much better and the eight sleeves of balls he sent were as much to memorialize their bond in bad golf as to jab him. The associate wrote back, "I am writing to confirm that you will send a twenty-fifth ball when I make my hole-in-one."

Walter's relational mastery was not limited to self-deprecation and service. He was also meticulous about research and numbers. He never attended a meeting—whether on a golf course or in a boardroom—without vetted metrics. Often before a prospective client could ask their questions, Walter had provided the answers. He would have made a crack attorney had he the stomach for half-truths. As it was, Walter preferred linear thinking mixed with strategic dashes of imagination.

This method was not only used for landing new clients. Ernst's current Japanese clients like Mikasa and Mitsubishi Electric quickly made Walter their *de facto* business advisor as he helped them grow their presence and profits on the West Coast. Walter knew that by being more than a number cruncher, he could offer a much higher return to the Japanese businessmen who didn't always understand the quirky mores of American culture, particularly in southern California.

For instance, the Japanese didn't fully comprehend the benefits of a business taking an active role in giving back to its community. Furthermore, they defaulted to keeping a low profile in the States, a carryover from being enemies of the U.S. in WWII. The notion of civic involvement seemed unnecessary, if not uncomfortable. Walter helped the Japanese businessmen see that not only had America moved on from the war, but also that civic service was an integral part of business growth. It engaged their customer base and, if done well, won their hearts. In other words, the by-product of betterment of their communities was a better bottom line.

Walter also convinced the Japanese businessmen of the flipside — if their communities were not healthy, they would become an anchor that pulled down every business in the area. These conversations took place most often over lunch at the California Club or on the L.A. Country Club golf course. The club grounds were like a Petri dish for hot topics, and Walter's message soon began to spread like an invisible organism. Before long it was a locker room topic among the WASP elite. To some, it was a threat. To others, a solution.

In 1974, the U.S. was suffering under a recession that would effectively bring an end to the post-World War II economic boom. While Los Angeles was on its way to surpassing Chicago as the nation's second most populous city, many of its big businesses were feeling the effects of the oil and steel crises. The stock market crash that lasted from January 1973 to December 1974 was merely confirmation of what everyone already knew. To survive, businesses would have to not only change some fundamental mechanics of commerce; they would also have to change how they fundamentally thought about business in the first place. Suddenly, Los Angeles businesses realized they needed a man at the city's helm who understood the changes that needed to occur and was ready to lead them. While Walter could do a lot, he also needed help. That's where Mayor Bradley came in.

Bradley had seen more opposition than support from downtown businesses upon his election. However, with the passage of his 1974 redevelopment plan, which included the placement of influential business leaders on important city committees, the tide began to change. The local businessperson now had a say in city development and growth.

By the end of 1975, the confluence of Walter's spreading message with Mayor Bradley's plan was like a two streams merging together to form a broader, faster river. Walter had a larger platform on which to spread his message. The mayor had a direct vein to the heart of the city's business elite.

On June 1, 1976, Walter was asked to deliver a speech to the Town Hall of California in downtown Los Angeles. He did not waste the opportunity. The title of his speech was "How to Be Ethical in an Unethical World: A Fundamental Guide for Business." Whether or not it was what the audience expected, it was precisely what they got, and then some.

"It certainly was an act of reckless courage on someone's part," Walter began, "to have selected an auditor as your speaker today. For some of you will recall Elbert Hubbard's damning description of the typical auditor as: 'A man past middle age, spare, wrinkled, intelligent, cold, passive, noncommittal, with eyes like codfish, polite in contact, but at the same time unresponsive, calm, and damnably composed as a concrete post or a plaster of paris cast. A human petrification with heart of feldspar and without charm of the friendly germ, minus bowels, passion, or sense of humor. Happily, they never reproduce and all of them finally go to hell.'"

Walter then confessed how odd it was to select an auditor to speak on ethics, "especially in view of how some businesses select their auditors." He then told them the story of the auditor who felt two and two equaled whatever figure the executives had in mind. When the laughter subsided, Walter took a slightly serious turn and shared what he called the real essence of ethics as evidenced in the story of the wealthy oil tycoon who built an Olympic-size swimming pool and filled it with crocodiles.

He was so delighted that he had a christening party to which everyone from miles around was invited. While the guests were enjoying drinks on the patio, the oilman then issued a challenge: if any unmarried young man would swim the length of the pool and survive the crocs, he would reward him with a choice of three things: a million dollars, a 10,000-acre ranch, or his daughter's hand in marriage.

Within seconds, a young man's body hit the water and there was a spectacular churning in the water for the next moment until, to everyone's amazement, the young man pulled himself out of the water at the other end of the pool without a scratch on him.

The oilman rushed to the young man's side. "I don't believe it!" he exclaimed. "There's no way anyone could survive those crocodiles, but here you are without a scratch on you."

The oilman then kept his word and offered then young man his choice.

Walking away, the young man said, "I don't want any of them. Really, I don't!"

The oilman grabbed the young man's arm and pulled him back.

"I am a man of my word," he said. "Now, which do you want? A million dollars, a 10,000-acre ranch, or my daughter's hand in marriage?"

"I don't want any of them!" retorted the young man. "All I want is the name of the bastard who pushed me into the pool!"

"Now that's the essence of ethics," declared Walter with a grin. "The young man could not accept the reward because it never was his intention to be a contestant."

Once the laughter subsided again, Walter entered the hearts of his audience. "In a very real sense, as a CPA ethics is my business...and, without question, the glue that maintains the individual and the greater society in an orderly relationship with each other... Maybe, just maybe, gentlemen, it is our moment; maybe we are that champion that is so desperately needed today."

For the next twenty minutes, Walter held court as he seamlessly weaved his message back and forth between an exposition on the current state of business in America to the charges of current and ancient voices calling businesspeople to take the higher road or face the consequences on which history has well-versed them. With each pause and paragraph, Walter's speech climbed to a climax.

"While business and businessmen had better get down to the serious business of building a better mousetrap and providing a superior service—and doing it devoid of deceit—politicians and public officials likewise had better accept their servanthood responsibilities and recognize that political expediency is inimical to public service.

"Somehow, we—all of us—must eradicate from society its warped sense of morality, which seems to hold that God ought to be thankful that we're living where we are and for keeping His economic place clean. If the family, the schools, society, and the church aren't going to issue a call for high moral and ethical standards, then business must... We must believe in another fundamental; namely, that all men are of one family, that the highest reaches of mutual concern and respect cannot be achieved unless there is a prior acceptance of kinship. Embracing this, then any act which would put another human being at a disadvantage would be strongly inconsistent and despicable as well. And if I believe that men are of one family, then it follows that I would empathize, for in the deepest sense ethics are the attitudes and rules we follow in dealing with one another. 'A man to be greatly good,' said Shelley, 'must imagine intensely and comprehensively; he must put himself in the place of another and of many others; the pains and pleasures of his species must be his own.'"

Fully aware of the growing weight of his words on the audience, Walter then began removing the weight, anecdote by anecdote, phrase by phrase, until all that remained when he was through was the burden laid upon each individual in the room, including him.

"At the same time, I would not apologize for profit. I would be proud of it. For money-making and doing the most good for the most people are not mutually exclusive.... And if we're proud of profit, let's communicate the economics process to *all* members of society....

"I don't hold with those prophets of doomsday who claim people are no good...or those cynics of despair who say, 'It doesn't really matter.' To the contrary, I hold with those who say, 'It really does matter.' Like Elbert Hubbard, 'I believe in the stuff I am handing out, in the firm I'm working for, and in my ability to get results. I believe that honest stuff can be passed out to honest men by honest means. I believe in working, not weeping; in boosting, not knocking; and in the pleasure of my job. I believe that a man gets what he goes after, that one deed done today is worth two deeds done tomorrow, and that no man is down and out until he has lost faith in himself. I believe in today and the work I'm doing, in tomorrow and the work I hope to do, and in the sure reward which the future holds. I believe there is something doing somewhere for every man ready to do it. I believe I'm ready…right now.'"

There was a brief pause after Walter finished, as though the audience had finally taken a breath. Then the applause rumbled from the front to the back of the room as attendees leapt to their feet. It was the beginning of something, perhaps a movement but, in the very least, a shift in the city's ethos.

On an individual level, Walter's stock rose both in the minds of those who were secretly frightened by his words, and in the minds of budding leaders who finally had an archetype to model. Tom Bradley was there, too. He was nodding.

***

Over the next two years, Walter practiced what he preached at the highest level. He believed in the truth of his own words—they were not mere rhetoric. Deep down, he also wondered about the prognosis he'd been given two decades before. The doctor had said he wouldn't live past his fifties and Walter had turned fifty just six weeks before the speech.

The celebration was held at a restaurant called Caves de Roy and forty close friends and family members attended. Once the partygoers were seated at their assigned tables, a crisp tenor voice rose from an inside stairwell against the north wall of the restaurant. Walter turned to see his favorite opera singer, Toni Dalli, stepping toward him and singing Sinatra's "My Way." Marrgo and Jan had flown him in from Italy for the occasion.

A cake fashioned into a red and white crown with fifty candles burning atop was wheeled to Walter's table. Dalli then led the room in an operatic round of "Happy Birthday." The first course of the meal was served and the evening meandered as memorable nights do, and bellies were filled with food and wine and laughter.

As the evening came to a close, Jan Burmeister, known now as the Beran's adopted daughter, stood and read a poem to Walter that was based on the story she'd heard of the old French woman from the war. Jan titled it: "To Walter – from your Dear Departed Friend."

Son, though I hardly knew your name,
Your face I can still clearly see today.
My Heart is warm because I also see
You listened to the things I had to say.

Our nightly conversations back in France
(Was it as long ago as '44?)
Gave this small solitary soul a chance
To Breathe my thoughts to one who'd use them more.

Remember, then, among our parting words
I asked in honor of what precious time
That you would wonder if I'd someday come
To reminisce and share a sip of wine,

Just as you then risked AWOL charges to come
And with this old woman spend your time,
I see you sacrifice one sip for me,
Despite your fervent love of quenching wine.

And as those swallows you have left behind
Have many times my cup of gladness filled,
So, in your greatness you have made me great
By being in your lifetime what I willed.

Avec Amour

It was the perfect ending to what was, noted Walter to Jan the following day, "the most fantastic evening of my life."

Walter rarely lacked inspiration, but his fiftieth birthday fanned the flame inside him to new heights. Whether he worried about the prophecy over his health is not known. If he said anything, he did so only to God in each early-morning time of prayer.

What is known is that Walter's portfolio of involvement became more diversified than any Los Angeles businessman of his time. In fact, a running commentary around the office was that Walter Beran was the required name in every committee directory. Besides being active in leadership roles with the Planning Committee of the American

Institute of CPAs, the California and Texas Societies of CPAs, and the National Association of Accountants, Walter taught adjunct business and finance courses at both the USC Business School and California Lutheran College and was on the Board of Councilors for the former. In fact, in the span of one week during the spring of 1978, he spent time with students at USC, Cal Lutheran College, and Brigham Young University, and he didn't just teach them. One student at USC was so moved by Walter's philosophy on business ethics he declared, "Mr. Beran for President!" Walter smiled. The student didn't know that becoming President was something Walter had dreamed of when he walked the cotton fields in The Grove.

If Walter's aforementioned commitments were not enough, he would also assume leadership roles with:

- The California Assembly
- The Los Angeles County Board of Supervisors
- The Skirball Cultural Center for Jewish heritage and American democratic ideals
- The Los Angeles Music Center
- The Los Angeles Jewish Big Brothers
- The Advisory Committee for the California State World Trade Commission
- The Senate Advisory Commission on Cost Control in State Government.

He also maintained regular involvement with non-profit organizations that were doing important work in the city, such as:

- The Salvation Army
- World Vision International
- Occidental College
- National Association for the Hispanic Elderly.

Most amazing about Walter's hyper-involvement is that he was, in fact, very involved. He wasn't merely a donor or honorary member or once-a-year meeting attendee. He lunched with key individuals. He invited them to his and Speedy's home. He took them golfing and introduced them to other influential businessmen in the city. Somehow, he still found time to invest in those closest to him, like Jan Burmeister whom he'd recently helped purchase a 1974 Mustang.

Others formulated their own descriptions of Walter and so he came up with an original one for himself. He was not, he insisted, a workaholic. He was an "involvaholic."

In 1977, The California Assembly and Los Angeles Country Board of Supervisors paid tribute to Walter for "outstanding community, philanthropic, and professional achievement." On June 8, 1978, Walter received an honorary Doctorate of Law degree from California Lutheran College for his dedication to its students. It was quite a mark he'd already made in such a short time. The stream of recognition seemed to flow annually from there, so much so that his "involvaholism" seemed like hyperbole.

Several years later, Jim was working in Washington D.C. for the Commerce Department in International Trade when he received a phone call from the Executive Assistant to the Secretary of Commerce, then Malcom Baldridge. The man explained they wanted to put Walter on the President's Export Council and asked if Jim could send over a résumé. Jim contacted Margo for the most current one and sent it to the Secretary's Office who then forwarded it on to the White House for approval and confirmation by President Reagan.

The next day, Jim's phone rang again. It was someone from the White House who handled the vetting of Presidential appointments and job placements. The man asked if he was Jim Beran and if Walter Beran was his father. Jim said yes. The man then explained that he had Walter's resumé in front of him.

"This résumé is bullshit," he asserted.

"Really?" Jim asked. "Why is that?"

"Because no one could possibly be involved in this many things at this level at the same time."

Jim didn't suffer fools gladly. He replied, "Why don't you walk your ass down the hallway to your boss's office [Assistant to the President for Personnel who knew Walter Personally] and ask him if it's bullshit. Then you call me back." Jim then hung up.

Ten minutes later Jim's phone rang. Now very apologetic, the man confessed, "I see a hundred résumés a day, and most are full of BS. I've never seen anything like this that was real."

***

In only six years, Walter's work was already swelling into something significant for Ernst and the city, although the results were not yet clear. Then in September 1978, he received a call from John while penning a final letter from the road for Speedy's next birthday album. Speedy had been rushed to the hospital with severe pain in her abdomen.

Walter's strength fell away. He called Marrgo, who quickly made arrangements for him to fly home. On the flight Walter composed the only letter with which he did not begin: "Dear Mrs. B."

September 27, 1978

Speedy,

How quickly the moment changes! Like with a flash of lightning a tree is downed, so too, quickly and devastatingly human life is changed. How well only you know how alone you must have been this morning. And how suddenly "my world" had no place to go, because I wasn't with you. All those occasions I have been away were but a moment compared to the agony of an eternity which I encountered when John—after much concerned effort—reached me by phone to tell me of your ordeal.

Since John's call, I have learned from you of the medical tests and examinations of today and tomorrow. How piercing the question: what does tomorrow hold?

All of a sudden, I never before realized how much an individual could be alone; and all of a sudden, all of those moments and hours and days I have been away have indeed become an eternity. All the moments become forever. How much one person can become so entwined in the rubrics of another's life—and one is not conscious of it until the threat of it being severed flashes piercingly in the heart and mind!

Yet, as these thoughts render one weak and seemingly helpless and defeated, there are currents which make one reach for a better reality and that is of the God who, in His mysterious wisdom and love, puts all things together. And the reality I know is that He will bring us beyond the ordeal of the present to a day of

110

gladness beyond. Jacob would not let the angel go until he blessed him; and tonight I won't let him go until he blesses us. So measurably have we been blessed 'til now that it would be a bad investment for Him not to continue. I know He will.

Walter's faith held firm, and a few hours later the doctors confirmed Speedy would need an appendectomy but nothing more. She would return to herself soon. The same could not be said for Walter.

Following Speedy's health scare, he made a firm decision in his heart. If he achieved the greatest impact the world had ever known but Speedy was not by his side, it would not mean nearly as much to him. Now more than ever Walter knew that the foundation of his strength was his faith in God, and God had chosen Speedy as the primary vehicle to confer his strength.

The holiday season of 1978 would signal a final change, an addendum, in Walter's dream. No matter what the financial cost or scheduling inconvenience, he would include Speedy in his work and, whenever possible, the boys too, and they would realize his dream together.

On December 20, Walter and Jim took a road trip down the coast of Baja California in Jim's Bronco. After getting run off the road by a large truck and taking on "minor damage," they finally arrived at their destination, a small town called San Quentin approximately 200 miles south of the border with a superb beach Walter described to Speedy as "wide, flat, and stretching out for miles." For two days, he and Jim made camp on the beach, enjoying long walks, fishing for their meals.

When Walter returned home, he and Speedy joined their friends for their annual Christmas dinner at L'Estrada. It would be the last dinner the quaint restaurant could contain.

The following Christmas of 1979, Walter asked Marrgo to plan the dinner for seventy-five guests. He invited the regular couples and then a host of others from their neighbors in Trousdale Estates, to Japanese businessmen Walter had grown to love, to school administrators and city officials. The dinner was held at the Caderoy Club ballroom on the first Sunday in December—a date which would become a permanent hold on the calendars of dozens of Los Angeles luminaries.

After 1979, the Christmas dinner was never again called a dinner. To attendees it was known as the Berans' Annual Christmas Party. To Walter it was something more. From the 1980s on, the party would serve as a measuring stick of Walter's impact on the city of Los Angeles.

1986

10

Broader

In 1924, Ernst & Ernst allied with the prominent British firm, Whinney, Smith & Whinney. It was a prosperous friendship that eventually broadened into something bigger. As Ernst continued to expand its client-base through international relations, Whinney, Smith & Whinney became an increasingly useful ally. In 1979, the two firms took the leap and merged forming the Anglo-American Ernst & Whinney and creating the fourth largest accounting firm in the world. Suddenly, Walter's field of opportunities was amplified. Ernst & Ernst had already established a solid national reputation, but the merger put Ernst & Whinney on the international map.

One of the regional accounts Walter fostered was the Atlantic Richfield Company, otherwise known as the oil and gas giant ARCO. Its vice president, Lod Cook, and Walter had become fast friends in a matter of a couple years. It was through that friendship that Walter came to meet the former governor of California and a fast rising presence in the political landscape—Ronald Reagan. The introduction between he and Reagan had not yet happened but after the merger, Lod made it known to both men that one was forthcoming.

In July 1980, Walter penned a congratulatory letter to Reagan upon hearing of his acceptance of the Republican nomination for president. A week later, Reagan wrote back thanking Walter and sharing his hope that through Lod they'd have the opportunity to meet very soon.

When Reagan won the election that fall, Walter was pleased. He wrote Speedy a note that he hoped the president elect would be the man he seemed to be on television. A few weeks later, Speedy retrieved their mail at 600 Clinton Place. In the middle of the stack of cards, invitations, and solicitations that always came that time of year was a handwritten note addressed to both her and Walter. It was from Nancy Reagan, inviting them to Washington D.C. for the president's inauguration on the twentieth of January. The Berans accepted and thus commenced a friendship that would bloom into something more than they expected.

Nancy and Speedy were like sisters from the start. They shared the same calm demeanor that paired nicely with leading men who were happy conducting conversations. The two women also shared an immense internal strength. During President Reagan's two terms in office, they didn't have as much opportunity to sit together as they would have liked. Instead, they exchanged letters on a regular basis, every couple of weeks.

Walter and the president were like boyhood friends. Reagan was fifteen years Walter's senior, but it never seemed true. They were like contemporaries stretched from the same cloth—men of high character and quick wit—and both carried themselves as though they had another fifty years to live. They also shared a love for Los Angeles, and they both had been touched by the Great Depression. This was their first topic of discussion when they finally met in person.

Walter recalled Reagan's 1976 "To Restore America" speech in which he explained, "Back in those dark Depression days I saw my father on a Christmas Eve open what he thought was a Christmas greeting from his boss. Instead, it was the blue slip telling him he no longer had a job. The memory of him sitting there holding that slip of paper and then saying in a half whisper, 'That's quite a Christmas present,' it will stay with me as long as I live."

Walter's boyhood in The Grove was wrought with similar memories as his mother sought to make ends meet and restore her broken life. He too knew the ache that accompanied that time in history.

However, the strongest bond they shared was their vision for their work. Each acknowledged having been ushered into the season of his life that offered the greatest opportunity for impact. It was a conversation that neither had been afforded—at least not comfortably—until they met. Yet in each others' presence and through each others' words, both men found great comfort in sharing personal burdens, challenges, and victories.

Neither man were politicians in the typical mold—but both were steadfast visionaries committed to seeing the future unfold as they believed it should and could be, and developing relationships with all parties involved was the key to realizing those possibilities. President Reagan aimed to build America into that "shining city on a hill" and Walter aimed to build Los Angeles into America's shining city. Ironically, the paths of both men would involve relations with other countries. While Reagan battled a former WWII ally in the Soviet Union, Walter befriended a former WWII foe in Japan. He believed that if Ernst, their clients, and Los Angeles were to continue growing, then expanding trade with the Pacific Basin countries—in particular Japan— was the path for opportunity for his company and his community.

***

On January 7, 1981, Walter was named the president of the Los Angeles Chamber of Commerce. The role came with a level of influence he knew was big if properly used. As Walter saw it, the position gave him a clear opportunity to assimilate and deliver his vision to the business world. The spark would begin in Los Angeles, but he hoped it would spread much wider than one city.

As Reagan proliferated his "Rescue America" speech to the nation during the first years of his term, Walter seeded his "How to Be Ethical in an Unethical World" speech to the local businesspeople and government officials of L.A. every chance he got. "Our compassion must become less institutional and more personal, particularly now that government is lessening its social role," he told a group of bankers and accountants.

Reagan and Beran were two men spreading their messages on two different plains of impact. Reagan's words were aimed at the masses in the hope that leaders would emerge. Walter's words were aimed at leaders in the hope that a movement would emerge. Both would make their mark in different ways and with the help of different key partners. Reagan had Margaret Thatcher. Walter had Mayor Tom Bradley.

While the two had crossed paths over the years since Mayor Bradley first heard Walter's speech in the Town Hall meeting — and while their mutual respect and admiration had grown over that same period of time as they followed each others' success and met informally on a couple of occasions — the mayor and Walter had yet to formally work together. They were friends, but had yet to combine their forces. That changed when the Mayor decided to run for governor of California in 1982.

Knowing Walter's trusted reputation in the business community, Mayor Bradley asked Walter for a meeting during which he requested Walter's advice in raising funds for his campaign.

Walter was a Republican and the mayor was a Democrat, so the motive of the question was not unclear—Walter advised many big businesses and Mayor Bradley was trying to understand the best way to tap into their resources.

Walter saw it differently. In truth, he saw the question in the way the Mayor intended it, but his belief in the integrity, leadership, and heart of the man compelled him to offer an answer the mayor hadn't expected.

Walter agreed to advise Bradley's staff on fundraising for his campaign, including making key introductions to businessmen he knew were supporters. In the end, it wasn't enough to usher the mayor to victory. On the night of the election, major news stations projected Bradley the winner only to discover that when the votes were counted, George Deukmejian had defeated the mayor by approximately 100,000 votes, or about one-percent of more than seven million tallied.

While the loss wouldn't affect the mayor's influence and ongoing work in Los Angeles, it was a disappointing political defeat and Walter knew it. Two days later, with the help of Speedy and Marrgo, Walter threw the mayor a party at the Beverly Wilshire. Between two pillars just inside the entrance of the ballroom a large banner was hung. It read: "We Still Love You, Tom." Five hundred people attended and Walter made sure they understood what sort of man he believed the mayor to be. "Tonight isn't about politics," Walter insisted from stage to open the night. "It's about celebrating one of the great leaders in our city."

Marrgo had arranged a big band to play songs from the 1920s, 30s, and 40s. Servers in black and white strolled the room with silver platters carrying *hors d'oeuvres* and drinks and, later in the evening, desserts. Bradley was all smiles as he made his way around the room, shaking hands, hugging, and conversing with friends. Walter watched the Mayor for much of the night and took pleasure in the mayor's pleasure.

From that evening on, the bond between Walter and Tom Bradley was soldered. Over the following two weeks, through phone calls and handwritten letters, the men sought a venture they could share. It was clear they held the same heart for the people of Los Angeles. The question was how they could put their heads together and do something even bigger than each could accomplish alone.

Two weeks later, Walter was riding the coastal train from San Diego back to Los Angeles. At a stop in North County San Diego, two immigration officers boarded the train and removed nearly a dozen Hispanic men who had obviously spent the day working on a construction site. He watched their faces fall and their heads bow in surrender. That night he told Speedy how his heart hurt for the men who were guilty of nothing more than trying to earn a living and put food on the table for their families. While Walter understood the officers were just doing their jobs, he wondered what message it sent to arrest people for working hard and making opportunities for themselves at no harm to others.

The fallen faces of those Hispanic men burned a memory in Walter's mind that would remain. He'd seen how hard such men worked when he was a young boy in The Grove. They took thankless jobs in the heat of the day for next to nothing and they never complained, nor did they ever do anything to hurt their fellow man. They deserved respect and they had his. Walter knew that, if not for the people of The Grove, the group on the train could just as well have included him.

***

By the early 1980s, Walter's work in the Japanese community had begun to gain traction. A major reason was what he would later call one of the smartest hires he ever made.

A young Japanese businessman named Yoshihiro Sano, Yoshi for short, was working for USC as part of a one-year international research MBA program. He was the Japanese business expert. Walter's continued involvement at the USC schools of business and accounting gave him an easy audience with the dean of the business school, whom he called asking for a lead on someone to help him take Ernst's Japanese interests further. The dean recommended Yoshi and handed Walter a slip of paper with his phone number. Walter called Yoshi the next morning and invited him to lunch at the California Club.

As usual, Walter received a few looks upon entering the club with an unqualified guest. He had come to expect the response, but it was no less unacceptable to him. He carried on with business. During the meeting with Yoshi, Walter commissioned him to develop a strategy for Ernst to expand its Japanese client base more rapidly. A few months later, thoroughly impressed by the strategy Yoshi presented, Walter hired him to help implement the strategy. As it turned out, Yoshi was not only a bright businessman, he was well connected throughout Japan. His strategy made an immediate impact.

Through his connections with Japan's Ministry of Foreign Affairs, the Embassy of Japan, and more specifically the Consulate General of Japan in Los Angeles, Yoshi began educating Walter on the key companies of various regions in his country. He explained how each should be approached given the varying cultural mores, from religious preference to family traditions to the proximity of the people in the community. He also fostered a solid relationship between Walter and the current Consul General of Japan living in Los Angeles. While he never said it, Yoshi was preparing Walter to be the *de facto* American consul general in Japan. Walter was a quick study and eager to see this branch of his vision take off before retirement, now about five years away.

To bolster their efforts, Yoshi put Walter in touch with Hugh Leonard, an Irishman who served as a Catholic priest in Japan for many years until he decided celibacy wasn't for him. He was now retired and living with his wife Ann in Los Angeles. Like Walter, Leonard was deeply committed to doing his part to strengthen the Los Angeles community on the whole. The two men connected at the heart level on this point. For the next two decades, they would develop a dear friendship that included working together on community projects and traveling together with Speedy and Ann.

One of the undying themes of conversation between them was Walter's commitment to excellence. Leonard saw this from the start when Walter asserted himself as an ideal student of the Japanese language. He came to love him for it; it also served as a ready source of humor when they were older and looking back. Walter studied Japanese daily, not just at planned intervals but also throughout the day, reciting common phrases as well as the Japanese word for various nouns he came across—a book, a car, a building, a man or a woman, a business. Walter also met with Leonard twice a week for eighteen months to receive ongoing instruction. He missed only one lesson in that span. As Hugh would later explain, Walter earned an A-plus for effort. Unfortunately, his nearly perfect attendance and unquestionable tenacity didn't translate into actually learning the language.

Around the eighteenth month, Walter abandoned the effort insisting that God must not have designed the German mouth to speak Japanese. Hearing him speak the common phrases brought a smile to Leonard's face—but not out of pride for his student's progress. Walter's pronunciation was so poor that even he could not understand some of the words. It was either clench his jaw or burst into laughter. Later, both would succumb to the latter.

With his pleasant appearance, impeccable manners, and Yoshi's endorsement, Walter still managed to communicate well enough to the Japanese business community and became instrumental in the expansion of Toyota, Mikasa, and Mitsubishi Electric in Los Angeles. In fact, Yoshi once told Walter that his greatest asset was that he "seemed Japanese."

What this meant, Yoshi explained, is that like the Japanese businessmen with whom he was meeting, Walter placed a high value on hard work and held to an inflexible standard of excellence. He was also an honest family man and he kept his word at all costs. It also didn't hurt, confessed Yoshi, that Walter was as short at 5'5 " than many of his Japanese associates" . With Speedy, at 5'1, The Berans were equally unimposing whenever they entertained as a couple.

During the same time another valuable friendship bloomed that came to expand Walter's desire and opportunity help his community. On a Saturday night during the spring of 1982, a respected inner city leader named Dr. Keith Phillips was preparing to be the guest preacher at the First Baptist Church of Beverly Hills the following morning. Just after dinner he received a call from the pastor of the church, Tom Stringfellow, who was a good friend of Walter's.

"I don't want to make your nervous," Rev. Stringfellow said to Dr. Phillips, "but Billy Graham is going to be in church tomorrow along with his friend Marvin Watson, the former Postmaster General."

Fortunately, Dr. Phillips had known the famous preacher as a boy. His father, Frank Phillips, organized some of the first Billy Graham

Crusades in Portland, Oregon in 1950. Having spent some time with Rev. Graham over the course of his childhood, Dr. Phillips was no stranger to the most famous preacher in America, but his presence in the audience was no less of an honor. He didn't know Marvin Watson or the other man Rev. Stringfellow had mentioned—a local businessman named Walter Beran.

After the service, Dr. Phillips joined Rev. Stringfellow, Rev. Graham, Marvin Watson, and Walter for lunch at the California Club. Dr. Phillips focused his attention on chatting with Rev. Graham and Mr. Watson, but as the lunch continued it became clear to him that Walter was someone with whom he needed to spend more time.

Walter's knowledge of the city's dynamics was surprising given he'd only lived there ten years. His heart for meeting the city's needs through good business and civic involvement also moved Dr. Phillips. Even though Walter didn't know it then, he was an answer to Keith Phillips' prayers. The timing was also fortuitous for the city.

Beneath the surface of Los Angeles's new economic prosperity, racial tensions still boiled. The growth was true but, like fresh sod over a sewer field, it was only a matter of time before a stench began to rise. One place where this occurred was in the city's prominent private clubs: the Jonathan Club, the California Club, and the Los Angeles Country Club, all of whom still maintained an unspoken intolerance.

It is both surprising and shameful that any such standard, unspoken or not, still existed in a city whose longstanding and well-respected mayor was black and whose people had already suffered through one racially-triggered tragedy in the 1960s. The standard still existed in the clubs nonetheless but by the 1980s, its strength was rapidly diminishing largely due to a growing and outspoken resentment of any such intolerance.

In the summer of 1982, the city put its foot down. The Los Angeles Community Redevelopment Agency told its employees they were banned from doing business at the Jonathan Club. Other city government agencies followed suit, followed by several local banks, law firms and businesses, including ARCO for whom Walter's friend Lod Cook was now the CEO. Cook went on record that he would no longer reimburse employees for memberships at the Los Angeles Country Club or the Jonathan Club.

If Walter's friends were on the front lines of the culture war, he was covertly inside the enemy camp. He continued conducting lunch meetings at the California Club and golf meetings at the Los Angeles Country Club, but he began to increasingly press the envelope as these meetings were increasingly with associates and friends that were neither Anglo-Saxon nor Protestant.

In numerous letters to Speedy, Walter continued to recall the disapproving looks from clubs' front desks. He also explained that he believed the bigger dream before him was too important to grandstand a core value—at least not yet.

It would be cliché to say Walter's vision continued moving at full steam if the description wasn't so literal. On July 27, 1983, he received a personal letter from Mayor Bradley thanking him for being instrumental in securing a passing vote to develop the Los Angeles metro rail project. Walter's ongoing leadership on boards and civic endeavors throughout the city—the body of which had expanded exponentially after his year as president of the Los Angeles Chamber of Commerce—earned him a level of influence with the city's luminaries such that his request carried enormous weight. The chief executive of a large bank summed up the ethos surrounding Walter when he explained that in the 1980s, if Walter Beran was behind something, that something was worth being behind. A 1983 survey of CEOs, public affairs officers, and city officials confirmed his assertion. The survey identified Walter as one of four "exceptional leaders" in Los Angeles who provided key direction to the business community. Case in point: construction would begin on the metro rail project a year and a half later.

If a train was not a fitting enough metaphor for the trajectory of Walter's influence, perhaps a torch was. In July 1984, Ernst & Whinney was named the official manager of the results system for the Olympic Games in Los Angeles. The event was not only a coup for the city; it was a personal coup for Walter. The opportunity gave him a chance to work closely with Peter Ueberroth, the former commissioner of Major League Baseball who was heading up the Olympic Committee, which afforded him the rare privilege of carrying the Olympic torch for a stretch.

As the big day approached, Walter's excitement was evident in a letter to Speedy.

July 19, 1984

The August 6th issue of Fortune came out today. As you turn the cover page, you can't help but see a sharp, color, double-page ad on E&W and its Olympic role. The ad is first class and so is its message. Part of the message reads, "It takes the professional performance of Ernst & Whinney, designated as Manager and Operator of the 1984 Olympic Results System." The best part reads, "E&W—Ernst & Whinney—and results. They go together." I like that because in most of life, which I have encountered, results are what count.

I'm delighted to see the impact our Olympic role is beginning to have on our organization. All our people the world over can identify with and relate to our role, and a number from around the world are going to be directly involved. I'm confident our people will perform beyond expectations. And, with super pride, I'll carry the Olympic Torch on Saturday.

The combination of Ueberroth's entrepreneurial acumen and Walter's accounting acumen made the 1984 Summer Olympics a big success on all fronts, but the one accolade that made Walter proudest—a fact he only admitted to Speedy—was that Los Angeles became the first host city to hold a profitable Summer Olympics since 1932.

Whether the symbolism was apparent to Walter at the time he didn't say, but in hindsight his involvement in the Olympics and, in particular, carrying the Olympic torch was a perfect snapshot of his life. He was less than two years from sixty and about to begin his second to last year with Ernst. The Olympic torch was not the only one he was carrying, nor was it the only one that would ignite a larger, lasting flame.

A good example was Walter's involvement with the Los Angeles Music Center, which housed three theaters that featured the world's leading opera singers, Broadway shows, and symphony orchestras. At the time, it was also a frequent host for the Oscars. Charles Schneider, then the group vice president of the Times Mirror Co., wrote to Walter on July 11, 1984 to thank him for his integral involvement in the Music Center's fundraising campaign that year. Walter served as campaign

chairman. Schneider addresses him, "Sir Walter" and then gushes
with praise:

> *Campaign '84 was, far and away, our most suc-*
> *cessful ever...over 11,000 donors whose gifts collec-*
> *tively total $7,637,529.... Up until now I thought it was*
> *I who worked the hardest and smartest when I had the*
> *responsibility you had this year. But, in honest, objective*
> *retrospect—it was you who may not have worked any*
> *harder, but surely worked smarter and, as the record*
> *attests, more than twice as effectively.... Bottom line,*
> *Walter—I am a genius because I got you involved.*

In 1978, Walter and Speedy had purchased a condo on the cliffs of
Capistrano Beach that was meant to eventually serve as their retirement home. Until 1984, it had served only as a rare respite. Its primary
purpose was acting as a storage unit for non-essentials, which included
Walter's growing library and wine collection.

During the fall of 1984, Speedy felt it needed a little more attention. She stayed at the condo alone and worked on making it more
homey while Walter and Yoshi took a six-day trip to Japan to discuss the dollar-yen relationship with several influential Japanese businessmen, including Tetsuzo Ota & Co, Japan's largest accounting firm
with whom Walter had spearheaded a merger earlier that year. Walter
also used the fall trip as an opportunity to visit Hiroshima, about which
he wrote to Speedy the night afterward.

> *November 4, 1984*
> *A moment to pause, and there aren't many places*
> *in the world to pause like Hiroshima, Japan. My early*
> *morning jog around the castle reminded me again what*
> *this place means to mankind.*
> *I pause, being reminded of many events and things,*
> *and of a favorite poem:*
>
> *I will grow old perhaps, but not today,*
> *Not while my hopes are young, my spirit strong,*
> *My vision clear — because life has a way*

Or smoothing out the wrinkles with a song!
I will grow old perhaps, but not today,
Not while my dreams remain a shining shield,
My faith a lance, and 'neath a sky of grey,
My colors wave upon the battlefield.
I will grow old perhaps, but not today,
Not while this pen can write upon a page,
And memories turn winter into May,
Shall this stout heart be brought to terms by age!
I will grow old perhaps, but not today,
And scorning time who would enlist my tears,
I stand convinced there is a better way,
Of occupying all the coming years.
I will grow old perhaps, but not today —
In my own style and in my own sweet time.
No night so dark there does not fall a ray
Of light along the narrow trail I climb.
O say of me, when my last hour slips
Like one bright leaf to softly rest among
The other... 'Life was honey on the lips
Of one who died believing he was young.

I would only add for myself that I wish to grow older,
but only as long as I generate youthful thoughts, dream
of better days, aspire to more enriching accomplish-
ments, and maintain a youthful spirit to pursue them
all, with you.

What Walter didn't say in his letter was that Yoshi had made a last minute decision to inform some of the local businessmen that a WWII veteran and prominent businessman from America would be visiting the Hiroshima Peace Memorial with him. Yoshi expected a casual meet and greet with a dozen people. Instead, 200 local business people showed up. It was a telltale sign of how far Walter's influence had reached into that society and how ripe the countries were for partnership.

Rather than turn the crowd away or attempt to meet every individual, Yoshi ran inside the building and retrieved an amp and a handheld microphone from a Memorial employee. He and the employee hurried them to a central location where Walter then spoke from his heart as Yoshi translated:

> *First, I'd like to express my thanks for this warm and unexpected welcome. I feel very much at home in your beautiful country. Second, it is impossible for me to describe the honor I feel for the opportunity to speak to you today. I was once a soldier in the United States Army who fought against this great country. I was young—only eighteen years old—and much has changed since then. I am now nearly sixty years old and the fact that I am here today, standing in your warm presence, beneath this poignant memorial is incredibly significant. In a sentence, it symbolizes that we have all become better people in time and that there is certainly a bright future between the United States and Japan...*

Walter spoke for twenty minutes, and when he finished the crowd erupted in applause. Four days later Walter and Yoshi were still in Tokyo discussing business when President Reagan won the election for a second term. Walter wrote to Speedy that he was hopeful Reagan's victory would mean better times for the U.S., and he described his time in Japan as an enormous success. When the trip was finished, he and Yoshi had all but secured relationships with Nippon Kokau and Isuzu Motors, Mitsukoshi Department Stores, and the Japan Automobile Manufacturers Association, with the support of Ernst's current partnerships with Mazda, Toyota, Nissan, and Isuzu.

When Walter returned home from his trip, Speedy handed him a poem that had come in the mail from Jan Burmeister. She was now living in what seemed like her tenth city since first moving into their home in 1973—Walter called her his "favorite gypsy"—but the Berans had remained in close contact. Jan's letter began with "Dear Mom and Dad II." Her subsequent words reveal her admiration:

Ode to Walter F. Beran

You'd want to win the world for him;
You'd want to make him smile.
His nod or his approval
Made the toughest task worthwhile.

The secret to his leadership
May be in servanthood,
For only by example
Is the grindstone understood.

So, if it seemed a pressure came
To you from time to time,
It's 'cause he knew, in order to
Turn good grapes into wine,

Required careful squeezing
And a bit of pungent yeast.

To Beran raise those glasses
And impart a thank-you feast!

October 1, 1985 marked the first day of Walter's last year with Ernst. His words to Speedy revealed a man mindful of the influence he'd already had and yet a man still focused on making a greater impact through a now-proven strategy:

> *If one desires to achieve a good thing, he should not neglect to pay attention to small things, for it is by the accumulation of small things that a great thing comes into being.*

On the evening of the first Sunday in December that same year, Walter and Speedy stood at the head of a long line of prominent guests waiting to greet them outside the Grand Ballroom of the Beverly Wilshire Hotel. The prominent men in their tuxedos and black ties and the prominent women in their fine gowns and complementing jewels had become a common sight for those who spent any time around Walter and Speedy. The luminaries in Los Angeles flocked to them and the attention was deserved.

When Ethel and Tom Bradley finally reached the Berans, the mayor leaned down and kissed Speedy on the cheek as Walter did the same to Ethel. Then the mayor turned to Walter and, grinning, said, "Surely this won't be the last year."

Walter smiled and replied, "I hope we'll be enjoying a Christmas dinner with you and Ethel during for the next twenty years!"

Dodgers owner Peter O'Malley and his wife Annette then approached and the couples greeted each other in the same manner as the Berans and Bradleys had. After a brief, cheerful exchange, Jane and Michael Eisner were next. Following them were the Sanos and then a few others from the Japanese business community. Then came the current mayor, Richard Riordan, and others from the political community. The line continued like this, with names anyone in Los Angeles would know but few as genuinely as Walter and Speedy and rarely in one setting like this. These were their people now. Ironically, so were the people of Poteet and The Grove. It would be a stretch to say that Walter and Speedy could have predicted this was where they'd be standing in that moment of time—he in his wool tuxedo and she in her navy satin gown, after nearly forty years of marriage, hosting the premier holiday event for the most influential people in Los Angeles.

Once his guests were inside the ballroom and seated, Walter stepped onto the stage and offered his annual welcome. "If you came to my home for Christmas dinner," he explained, "we would begin with a blessing. So I've invited my friend, Dr. Keith Phillips, to offer that blessing before we begin our evening together."

The crowd bowed their heads with Walter, whether Christian, Catholic, Jewish, Buddhist or Muslim. Those who had not yet taken their seats stopped midstride. They closed their eyes and dropped their chins. Dr. Phillips closed his eyes and thanked God for the miracle of Christmas and for the year behind them and the blessings it brought. He asked for grace and protection in the year to come, and he offered his gratitude on behalf of all in the room who were fortunate enough to live in a free and prosperous country.

Following the prayer, Walter asked the room to stand and face the flag placed in the corner of the ballroom. He then led them in the Pledge of Allegiance.

He had come a lifetime from the cotton fields and the five-dollar-a-month shanty and the tragedies of The Grove and the War, but he'd not forgotten his story. As he looked at the American flag, he was again reminded of those dreams he had when he was a small boy. He put in the work and he'd been a benefactor. He later told Speedy that his heart was filled with as much joy and gratitude that night as he could remember.

After the Christmas party and a brief holiday vacation at home, Walter finished out his final nine months at Ernst with a bang. With the daily encouragement of his bride of thirty-seven years, he worked tirelessly to prepare the company to thrive without him and, as he put it to Speedy, help them avoid being "about where we are today." That largely meant ensuring Ernst could continue to broaden its ability to serve the Pacific Basin. It also meant ensuring Los Angeles would continue to flourish both above the surface and beneath it.

Beyond serving his key accounts well, Walter pooled his resources in the role of campaign chairman to raise funds for the Los Angeles Area United Way. The organization was facing the largest shortfall it had ever experienced. When the final tally came in, the organization had raised a record $85.5 million in pledges—$7.3 million more than any previous year and the highest total of any citywide campaign in the history of the organization.

Walter's secret was no secret at all. He now had entrée into the offices of nearly every prominent person in the city, and he was better than anyone at convincing people to care about more than money.

Marrgo would set up the meeting and Walter would walk in and present the opportunity. On one occasion, he was having lunch with Keith Phillips and brought him along to meet with the chief of Bank of America. Walter stepped inside the man's office, shook his hand, and immediately told him why he was there. "I'm giving my own money," Walter concluded, "and I'd like you to contribute as well."

The CEO didn't flinch. It wasn't the first time Walter had approached him for support and he knew it wouldn't be the last. But if Walter Beran was behind the cause he knew it was a cause worth supporting and it would not only be good for the community, but for the company as well.

"Okay," he replied as he reached for a pad of paper. "How much?"

Los Angeles Olympics, 1984

Atomic Bomb Memorial, Hiroshima Japan

11

And Then

Leaning into his final week of retirement, Walter recounted to Speedy the story he and a small group of fellow 12-13 year-olds were told in The Grove on the day of their Lutheran confirmation.

> *A father asked his son what he planned to do in life. The son answered, "Go to college."*
>
> *The father replied, "And then?"*
>
> *The son thought again and answered, "Become a teacher."*
>
> *The father promptly replied, "And then?" On this went. After each subsequent answer the son gave, the father would again ask, "And then?"*
>
> *Finally the conversation reached the point where it became obvious the ultimate meaning of the question was a transcendent one: What will you do if you were to do it for an eternity?*

Walter had his answer: The same thing he'd been doing all along.

It's been said that the truest measure of a man is in what he does when he's already done enough. By September 30, 1986, Walter had already done enough. It was his final day with Ernst & Whinney, who required their employees to retire at sixty, and by the most basic accounting measurement, he'd left an indelible mark on the company.

Since the year Walter took over the Western Region, revenues had increased in that region by a multiple of seven.

Now it was time to enjoy the twilight years with Speedy. He asked Marrgo for one final favor. A day later, she delivered a box of new business cards to him. In the center was his name with (RETIRED) beneath it. In the top left corner the cards read: "No Phone" and "No Address." In the bottom left the cards read: "No IRS" and "No GAAP" (which stands for Generally Accepted Accounting Principles). In the top right they read: "No Partners" and "No Clients." Finally, in the bottom right the cards read: "No Cleveland" and "No Meetings."

Walter had plans to finally read all the books he'd been saving and enjoy the fine wine he'd been collecting since San Antonio.

Five days after his final day at Ernst, Walter's penned one last letter to Speedy—letter number 1,771 over a twenty- two year span. In it, he expressed his excitement for their new life that lay ahead. He also alluded to the fact that while he'd accomplished much, it was not "the end of the story."

October 5, 1986

Mrs. B.,
Happy Birthday!
The magnitude of our experiences over the years covered by these notes have been fantastic. The most fantastic has been the people we've come to know as colleagues and friends. During those years we've come to know John and Jim in very special ways... To name them all would be endless....

Where does all this leave us, in terms of retirement?
I feel real good about it. Although I'd be less than honest to say that there aren't a couple of skeptical moments from time to time. There are some things I've wanted and tried over the years and missed. Like being president of the United States, or professional football's greatest player. But as the song goes, "Regrets, I've had a few; But then again, too few to mention."

I don't expect retirement is the end of the story, although I'm both ready and willing to accept the fact that it's the end of a chapter. I think that you and I will have a few moments now to discover that perhaps we can enjoy an exciting time in the daylight together just as we have a lot of evenings together, after dark...

So Speedy, whatever happens in our retirement, and whatever you think of it, I will love you...

> *As long as there is time,*
> *As long as there is love,*
> *As long as there is you,*
> *And as long as I have a breath to speak your name...*
> *I will love you,*
> *Because I love you more than anything in all the world.*
> *So don't fret!*
> *Look up!*
> *Take courage!*
> *We have a lot going for us. Let's go for it!*

No one knew better than Speedy and Marrgo that retirement would not stop the man who coined the term "involvaholic." The ladies had invitations printed for his retirement party and at the top they read:

"In Celebration of Walter Beran's Retirement...But Not Really"

Even President Reagan knew better. In response to his and Nancy's invitation, he wrote:

> *I am delighted to join with those gathered to con-gratulate you on your retirement as Vice Chairman of Ernst & Whinney. This is only one in a long list of accomplishments.... I think you said it best when you called yourself an "involvaholic." Few can boast of such a record of dedication, and I have a feeling that retirement from Ernst & Whinney only means you will pursue other avenues of service to your fellow citizens.*

Reagan was spot on. Post-retirement, Walter kept an office at the Ernst & Whinney Los Angeles headquarters and served as a part-time consultant to his former firm while he continued his quest. He rose at 4:00 AM to read Scripture and pray as he always had. He continued to jog five days a week. His favorite plaque remained on his desk that read: "All things come to he that waiteth as long as while he waiteth he worketh like hell."

Had Walter taken his final breath on October 1, 1986, he would have rested in peace knowing he'd done all he could do, knowing he'd carried out his vision to the best of his abilities during the moments he'd been given. Nevertheless, if God was willing to give him a few more years, he wanted to see the fruit of his labor as much as he could.

Four years before Walter's retirement, Keith Phillips' organization World Impact built the Los Angeles Christian School to serve inner city children. In many ways, the school was a culmination of Dr. Phillips' lifetime of dedication to the inner city youth of Los Angeles. The goal was to begin by offering kindergarten and first grade and then add a grade every year thereafter. By the time Walter had retired, it was time to build a junior high school in order to matriculate the kids graduating from sixth grade to a campus with a consistent curriculum. Walter offered to raise money by holding a fundraising luncheon at the California Club, where he still maintained a membership.

The details were ironed out and the key prospective donors were invited. On the day of the luncheon, Dr. Phillips showed up to the California Club as planned with a busload of black middle school boys from Watts with whom World Impact had been working for several years. They were good kids who'd worked hard to get out of the gang lifestyle and turn their lives around and Walter had supplied every one of them with suits. Dr. Phillips escorted the boys from the bus to the front door of the club.

The man acting as host took one look at the group and said, "I can't let you guys in." Keith assured him they were all guests of Walter Beran and suggested the man call Walter because he set the luncheon up. The man nodded and picked up the phone.

Before that day, Dr. Phillips had never once heard Walter raise his voice. The moment the California Club employee told Walter he couldn't let Phillips and the busload of boys into the club, Walter started yelling at the man with such volume that Dr. Phillips could clearly hear him say, "If you don't let those kids in right now I will call Otis Chandler [the publisher of the *Los Angeles Times*] and this story will be front page news tomorrow morning!"

"Yes sir," the man replied, and hung up the phone. Without another word, he opened the doors to the club and ushered Dr. Phillips and the middle-schoolers to the room Walter had reserved.

As they made their way, the kids' heads were on swivels and their eyes were wide with wonder over the high, vaulted ceilings and tall wooden columns. It was a world they didn't know existed and when Walter arrived shortly thereafter, he explained why he invited them.

"Look around, boys," he began. "All of this is not out of your league. It represents what you can achieve someday if you work hard and make good choices. I invited you here because I wanted you to see what is possible for you.... I believe in each one of you. I know you can all be great men!"

One night a few weeks after the fundraising luncheon, Walter was driving through a poor section of downtown with Dr. Phillips in the passenger seat when he spotted a young black boy of no more than eight or nine years old standing on the corner of an intersection. He was selling candy bars for his football team. It was around 10:00 PM. Walter pulled the car to the curb and rolled down the passenger window.

"How many do you have left to sell?" Walter called to him.

"Sixteen," the boy answered.

Walter pulled out his wallet and counted out enough money to buy them all. He called the boy over to the window and handed him the money.

"Now promise me you'll go straight home."

"Yes sir," the boy said as he handed the box of remaining bars through the window.

Walter pushed the box back to the boy. "You keep those and share them with your family," he said

A huge grin came over the boy's face.

"Really?" he exclaimed.

Walter nodded.

"Just promise me you'll go straight home."

The boy nodded, said thank you, and then took off running toward his house.

Walter pulled from the curb and returned Dr. Phillips to his house. Then, as he returned to his own home, Walter solidified an idea he'd been carrying for several months. The interaction with the boy selling candy was the final nudge. Perhaps he saw himself in the boy, doing whatever he could to make some money from patrons of The Grove. Perhaps the boy reminded him of the exasperating phone call with California Club host a few weeks earlier. Whatever emotion coursed his veins, it was the inspiration that moved Walter to action.

In the weeks that followed, with the support of local Japanese executives, Walter began planning an alternative from the storied but stubborn Los Angeles country clubs. They would build a new club that was open to individuals of any race, creed or gender. Walter explained to Mayor Bradley that he saw the club like an African watering hole, a place where at the end of each day the animals that had all tried to kill each other now gathered together and shared a drink.

***

While the City Club's construction was underway, Walter received a call from his old friend Lod Cook, who had accepted the position of acting chairman of the Ronald Reagan Presidential Foundation. Lod had an invitation for Walter. The Foundation was moving toward the financing and construction of the Ronald Reagan Presidential Library in Simi Valley, forty miles outside downtown Los Angeles. The venture needed the financial stewardship of an accounting sage. Would Walter consider being on the board as treasurer?

There was nothing for Walter to consider. His position was made official shortly thereafter. When the president and Nancy heard that Walter was coming on board, they had another request. Would he consider being one of the three executive committee members? Again, there was nothing to consider. Walter said yes with much gratitude, but he did not know the extent of the honor that had been bestowed on him until he attended the first executive committee meeting shortly thereafter.

There he looked into the faces of the only other members: Nancy Reagan and Nancy's best friend Mary Jane Wick. He told Speedy that night that the trust the Reagans had put in him was the highest honor he received in his life. As he'd been doing for four decades, Walter then took on his responsibilities as accountant and consultant with the utmost effort and integrity.

Construction of the library began in the second half of 1988 at nearly the same time that crews began renovating the top floor of the

Wells Fargo Tower at 333 S. Grand Avenue. The latter would soon be home to Los Angeles's newest club: The City Club on Bunker Hill. Before its doors would open on April 1, 1989, more than seventy-percent of the memberships had already been reserved at a $4,000 initiation fee.

When the doors finally opened, Walter escorted the club's first guest through its doors to a special room that carried his namesake: the Tom Bradley Room. A huge smile came over the mayor's face. He reached over the put his arm around Walter and he nodded and looked around the room. Finally, there was a club at which he felt welcome.

The Ronald Reagan Presidential Library was dedicated on November 4, 1991. It marked the first time in U.S. history that five presidents gathered in the same place: Nixon, Ford, Carter, Reagan, and George H. W. Bush. Just fifteen months later, under Walter's capable guidance, the final $2 million payment was made on the $57 million complex—the nation's most expensive presidential library at the time. The money for the 153,000-square-foot center, reported the *Los Angeles Times*, originated largely from "wealthy friends, big business, and Japanese interests." Many knew what that really meant—Walter Beran had been involved.

It was through the same Japanese interests that Walter's harvest came to bear more fruit. During the late 1980s, Walter also became the chairman of the board of the Japan America Society of Southern California. The position established him as the city's *de facto* business ambassador and gave him reason to take a second trip to Japan with Yoshi Sano. This time Yuki Togo, the head of Toyota Motor Sales, U.S.A. joined them. They toured the Tsutsumi plant in Toyota City, at which time Walter learned of the company's plans to launch their luxury vehicle cars in the States very soon. They named the brand "Lexus."

To that point, no one but Toyota employees knew of the plans as the company had kept their flagship sedan project, code-named "F1," under wraps. When Walter learned of the new luxury cars, he took out his checkbook, signed a blank check, and handed it to Yuki who knew precisely what to do with it.

Four months later, Walter joined Yuki again, this time at the Toyota Motor Sales, U.S.A.'s headquarters in Torrance, California, for the official unveiling of the first Lexus in America. At Yuki's request, Walter and the 22nd Ambassador to Japan, Jim Hodgson, were to be the guests of honor. The ceremony commenced and a white LS400—the first one sold in the U.S.—was unveiled to the audience's delight. The car had been six years in the making, noted Yuki. Then he spent a few moments describing the sedan's distinctive accessories and capabilities.

By the time Yuki was ready for the special presentation that followed, Ambassador Hodgson still had not arrived. Walter took the stage and stood beside Yuki, who scanned the audience one final time. When he didn't see the ambassador, Yuki looked over at Walter, shook the two sets of car keys in his hand, and shrugged.

"I guess these just go to you, Walter," he said with a grin. Then he handed Walter the set of keys to the white LS400 sitting beside them. (Ambassador Hodgson later received the keys to the second LS400 sold in the U.S.). When the applause died down, Yuki offered a brief send-off to those in attendance including Walter, whom he praised for helping establish the Lexus brand in the U.S. Then he dismissed the crowd with his customary call to action: "Sell like hell!"

Within a matter of weeks, Walter had a matching LS400 for Speedy, and two personalized plates that read ZEAGLE and ZEAGLES.

Birds of a feather

12

A Rare Vintage

It was through a conversation with Yuki Togo on Walter's second trip to Japan that he became intrigued by the Chinese economy. He believed there were signs of it being the next Japan in terms of economic explosion. Shortly thereafter, in 1990, Walter took a trip with Jim to see the country firsthand.

They toured Guangzhou (formerly Canton), Shanghai, Beijing, and Xian. Walter noted the signs of the country's growing economy to Jim at each locale, explaining what he thought that would mean in the next ten to twenty years. "But," he confessed, "I probably won't be around to see it."

At one point they were driving through the countryside of Xian, where the Terracotta Army resides, when they came upon dozens of large grass mounds that once served as tombs. Jim pulled the rental car over to the side of the road and suggested they climb one mound that was particularly large.

Walter was game and they hopped out of the car. Jim immediately took off running and bounded to the top in a matter of minutes. Jim turned around once he was at the top, expecting to see his dad's white Lexus hat bobbing up the final steps. Instead, Walter was only halfway up the mound.

"C'mon!" Jim called out playfully. "What's taking you so long?"

Walter didn't answer. He kept his head down and kept climbing. As he finally neared the top two minutes later, Walter replied, out of breath and with little emotion, "I'm not a young guy like you are."

Jim realized in that moment that his dad was aging. Even Walter Beran was mortal.

***

In December of the same year Walter, who was now seventy-four years old, stood on a stage in the Los Angeles Biltmore Hotel ballroom in front of a crowd of 700. Next to him stood a man named Taizo Watanabe, former consul general of Japan in Los Angeles and a man whom Walter considered a dear friend. Taizo and Walter met through Yoshi Sano and had become key allies in igniting the Japanese corporate movement in Los Angeles. Now the two men were being honored for their consummate achievements. However, they were sharing the stage that particular night for a more poignant reason.

As the host reminded the crowd, it was Pearl Harbor Day and on that fateful morning in 1941, the two men on stage were moving in opposing directions. Eventually, Walter's ship would be torpedoed by a Japanese ally and Taizo would witness his brother commit suicide in the aftermath of Hiroshima. That was now past. On December 7, 1990, the two men stood beside each other as colleagues and close friends who had accomplished something great together.

As the hostess finished her speech, Walter looked over at Taizo with a kind smile.

"I guess we really did get something started here," he said.

Taizo gave a big smile and nodded.

The host lifted her glass in a toast, and the crowd and its two honorees joined in.

It was a night to remember. It was also a night that would sadly serve as only half the picture of Los Angeles. While two former enemies in war living on two different continents raised a glass and toasted their shared prosperity, two groups of people sharing the same nationality and living within the same city limits had not yet found peace. Less than two years later, another civil war would erupt.

On April 29, 1992, a trial jury acquitted four Los Angeles police officers of assault and use of excessive force on a black man named Rodney King, whom they'd pulled over following a high-speed chase. Thousands throughout Los Angeles were enraged by the acquittal and began rioting. This time the bedlam was not limited to the inner city.

Homes and businesses in wealthy Hancock Park and Hollywood were smashed up and looted. The destruction was greater than the Watts Riots forty years earlier. When the chaos finally subsided six days later, fifty people were dead and property damage exceeded $1 billion.

In the wake of the devastation, Mayor Bradley consulted with Walter on the best course of action. In a subsequent conversation, the mayor asked if Walter would head up the Rebuild LA initiative. Walter told the mayor he would continue to support the efforts in whatever ways he could, but that he was not the right man to formally head up the effort.

"You need a younger man, Tom," Walter insisted. Walter was now sixty-six years old.

When he was home later that day, he told Speedy that the other reason he didn't accept the position was that he sensed all sides involved in the chaos lacked the political will to do what was necessary. As a result, the committee would fail and he'd "get arrows from both sides." Then he explained that ultimately he felt he could better serve the city by continuing to do what he was doing—hands and feet on the streets.

While Mayor Bradley was trying to forge a political path for the city's recovery, leaders of the Crips, a violent south-central Los Angeles gang formed when two gangs united, forged their own path. They walked through the doors of the World Impact offices and asked Dr. Phillips if he could arrange a meeting with some successful business people in the city. They wanted advice on how to fix their neighborhoods, which were in shambles.

"It's too late for us," one of the leaders asserted. "But we want to know how to make things better for our kids."

Choosing to confide in Dr. Phillips was deliberate. The gang leaders knew about his decades of work in their neighborhoods. They trusted him, and they didn't trust the LAPD or the city officials. They felt that businessmen were their last hope and if Dr. Phillips knew the businessmen, they could trust them. They reasoned that the hardworking, money-making businessman would understand them best if anybody could, if only because they shared an entrepreneurial inclination.

Dr. Phillips set up a meeting at the Imperial Courts recreation center in Watts. In preparation, he asked Walter to bring together the key business leaders in the city, including, Mayor Tom Bradley .

At the meeting, Beran and Mayor Bradley agreed to spearhead a fundraising campaign to help with the creation of an annex site of the Los Angeles Christian School. It would be called the Watts Christian School and it would be built near the Imperial Courts housing projects.

One prominent chairman in the city offered to do a fundraising luncheon at his company's offices. Walter made sure everyone was there, including local sports luminaries like Lakers owner Jerry Buss and Dodgers owner Peter O'Malley. When the day was done, nearly $1 million had been raised for the Watts Christian School. Construction began immediately thereafter.

As the day approached on which the Watts Christian School was to be dedicated, Walter and Mayor Bradley made sure all prominent city officials, the national press, and local TV were invited. However, when the day arrived, not one media outlet, city official (other than Bradley), or one local journalist showed up. Phillips, Bradley, and Beran stood on a makeshift stage before only those local businessmen who'd given their money and a few local families whose kids were to attend the school. When he realized what had occurred, Bradley looked at Dr. Phillips and Walter and said in a muffled voice, "If we'd been rioting, they'd have come in droves. When we do something right, they stay away."

Dr. Phillips nodded.

Walter looked at the faces of those in attendance. He knew the work they'd done still mattered, even if the media didn't see it that way.

***

Later that year, Walter would once again have a brush with death. Since leaving office, former president Jimmy Carter, through the Carter Center, had been engaging in humanitarian efforts throughout the world. One of his initiatives was to "advance democratic elections and governance consistent with universal human rights." Walter was invited by Carter to be an election observer in Guyana, South America. On Election Day, October 5th, observers were to assess the casting and counting of ballots.

When the day arrived, Walter was assigned a driver and a list of voting locations to observe and report. About halfway through the list, Walter and his driver headed for another polling location along a road that was unpaved and wound through remote jungle. At one point they came upon a tree lying across the road.

The driver stepped from the car to move the tree and was immediately surrounded by a group of armed robbers. With guns drawn, they ordered Walter out of the vehicle. The driver attempted to intercede and was pistol whipped to the ground. Walter was at a loss. He opened the pack that was around his waist in hopes of distracting them from the driver. He immediately produced a flashlight and shined it into one of the robber's eyes. The man cocked his gun, shoved it into Walter's face, and began to scream at him in Spanish.

"You can kill me if you must," Walter said calmly, "just don't shoot me in the face."

The robber continued yelling as Walter fumbled through his pack until he found his wad of cash—approximately $2,000.

Walter tossed it on the ground and the robber snatched it up. Immediately, he and the others disappeared into the jungle.

Beaten and bruised, the driver was well enough to continue. Shaken and thankful to be alive and not shot in the face, Walter would wait to return home before imparting the encounter to Speedy. As they continued to the next polling location, it occurred to Walter that one thing had not changed since World War II: spreading democracy was a dangerous business.

***

Four years later in the very same ballroom where he and Taizo Wantanabe had been honored, Walter was presented with the Japan America Society of Southern California's highest honor, the Kokusai Shimin Sho or "International Citizen's Award." Other recipients of the Kokusai Shimin Sho include: Japanese Prime Minister Yasuhiro Nakasone; California Governor Pete Wilson, Dr. Shoichiro Toyoda, chairman of Toyota Motor Corporation; Philip M. Condit, chairman and CEO of The Boeing Company; Minoru Makihara, chairman of Mitsubishi International Corporation: and Richard Rosenberg, chairman and CEO of Bank of America.

The following year, Walter was asked to head up the planning and guest list for a VIP dinner for Their Majesties, The Emperor and Empress of Japan. They would arrive first in Washington, D.C. and attend a dinner there before traveling to Los Angeles and the Beverly Wilshire hotel.

Every living Los Angeles dignitary hoped to receive an invitation but the guest list was limited—and Walter was the gatekeeper. He landed on a simple criteria for composing the list of distinguished invitees: they had to live and work in Los Angeles proper and care deeply about the future of the city. Walter invited the past and present mayors Yorty, Bradley, Riordan, and their wives. He invited the past and present governors Deukmejian and Wilson, and their wives. He invited his key Japanese business constituents: the Honorable James Hodgson; the Honorable Seiichiro Noboru, current consul general of Japan; Hiroshi Kawabe, president of the Japanese Chamber of Commerce of Southern California; and Takashi Kiuchi, president and CEO of Mitsubishi Electric US. Finally, Walter invited business titans like Michael Eisner of Disney, Robert Erburu of the Times Mirror Company, Lew Wasserman of MCA, Lynda and Stewart Resnick of The Franklin Mint, and John Petterson of Tiffany & Co. All confirmed their attendance.

ARCO chairman Lod Cook served as the dinner chairman and offered opening remarks, welcoming the Emperor and Empress of Japan. Following him were remarks by Mayor Richard Riordan, Yvonne Brathwaite Burke, chair of the L.A. County board of supervisors, and Governor Pete Wilson.

The Emperor of Japan then took the stage and offered a formal response in gratitude for the hospitality he and the Empress had been shown. The guests were then serenaded by the Los Angeles Children's Chorus while they enjoyed a four-course meal complemented by either a fine chardonnay or cabernet. Walter enjoyed the cabernet and in keeping with the promise he'd kept for some fifty years, he left a sip in the bottom of each pour.

Prior to the dinner, Walter's guests were allowed to pose for pictures with their Majesties. They lined up and one by one and the photographer snapped the shots. It was all very formal and the royal couple remained stoic the entire time, not cracking even the smallest grin.

When it was time for Walter and Speedy's photo, they stepped beside the royal couple and Walter whispered something under his breath to the Emperor. No one else heard it, but some later joked that Walter probably tried to say something in Japanese. Whatever it was, it tickled the Emperor. Suddenly his Majesty broke into a huge grin that turned into laughter as the photographer snapped off a series of candids.

Upon seeing this transpire, a Secret Service agent who'd been traveling with their Majesties leaned over to a young employee of the Japan America Society of Southern California and said, "That's the first time on this trip the Emperor has laughed."

***

Walter never lost that spark inside him. However, his body was failing him, much like his friend Ronald Reagan, who on June 5, 2004, lost his ten-year battle with Alzheimer's disease. Two days later, Reagan's casket lay in repose in the lobby of the presidential library that bears his name, as Reverend Michael Wenning, the Reagans' pastor at Bel Air Presbyterian, led a private family service. When the service concluded, Nancy approached the casket and laid her head on it. Walter and Speedy were there, and so was John, who had become a successful real estate broker in San Diego, and Jim, who finally had taken the advice of his dad and served in the Reagan White House and the Commerce Department before being named Director of Operations for the General Services Administration, supervising 12,000 Federal employees. Silent tears fell from all their faces.

After the private service, the library doors were opened to the public for the remainder of that day and the next. Then on the morning of June 9, Reagan's casket was loaded onto Air Force One and transported to Washington D.C. for the national funeral procession.

When Nancy Reagan returned home a week later to lay her husband's body to rest in Simi Valley, she placed a phone call to Walter and Speedy. Speedy answered and offered her condolences. But words were few in their inability to capture the essence of a loss so great. Two days later, a military official knocked on the Berans' door and presented Walter with a gift from Nancy. The official placed the small box in Walter's hand, saluted him, and then went on his way.

Walter looked down at the box and emotion came over him. He gathered himself and opened it. Inside was one of the shells from the 21-gun salute. Margaret Thatcher was among the other twenty friends of the former president to receive one. Walter considered it the greatest gift he'd ever received outside the blessing of his own family.

That gun shell was one of the last memories Walter's mind would allow him to treasure. While scarlet fever didn't kill him as a child, he learned it was the likely cause of his weak heart. It had given him almost three decades more than any doctor said it would, but by the time Walter was 77, his aortic heart valve had gone bad and needed to be replaced. The major surgery was successful, but the cumulative damage of a small depletion of oxygen to his brain over so many years had taken a toll. The result was what is known as as vascular dementia.

Over the next three and a half years, Walter's mental faculties began to fail him. Jim became his primary caretaker and, on many days, Speedy's too. Her heart was breaking as she watched her rock of nearly sixty years crumble before her.

Six months before Walter's death, Jim received a call from the executive director of the Reagan Foundation. His words began slowly, and the pain in his voice was evident.

"Jim, this is really hard for me…but as you are aware, your father's position as Treasurer has certain legal requirements…"

Jim stopped him there.

"You don't have to say anymore, I'll have a resignation letter for you today."

Nothing had ever hit Jim so hard, and now he had to help his dad find the words to say goodbye to one of the highest honors of his life.

With pen in hand, Jim put himself in the place of his father:

December 1, 2006

The Honorable Fredrick J. Ryan, Chairman
And fellow Members of the Board
The Ronald Reagan Presidential Foundation

Dear Fred and fellow Members of the Board,

I have been honored in my life to work and serve with many tremendous groups and individuals. But none have honored me and humbled me as with the blessing it has been to serve The Ronald Reagan Presidential Foundation, Former President Reagan, Nancy, and you, my fellow Board Members. For a small boy from a cotton patch town in Texas, it has indeed been "high clover."

But now the time has come for me to resign my position as Treasurer of the Ronald Reagan Presidential Foundation effective today, December 1, 2006. I hope to continue to serve the Foundation and the noble ideals of President Reagan that we seek to foster as long as the Lord permits.

With Deepest Regards,
Walter F. Beran

Holding back tears, Jim walked the letter into his father. Walter looked at the letter and then up at his son. With a small smile, he said, "Thanks, son."

Eventually, Jim was forced to entrust Walter to a home where he could be watched by professionals around the clock. His father was incoherent and his speech was gone.

Jim moved Speedy into the family home in Venice and they visited Walter every morning and afternoon, for hours at a time. It was a painful task, but one that no one questioned. He deserved their honor, even if he was no longer the giant of a man who changed the lives of everyone who knew him.

This man who ultimately helped alter the course of the second largest city in America died of respiratory failure on June 2, 2007, while surrounded by those he loved the most—Speedy, John, and Jim. Walter Beran was 81 years old.

It is perhaps no coincidence that his heart never gave out. Not even as he took his final breath.

The Great Wall

With President Carter in Guyana 1992

Epilogue

Fourteen years before his death, Walter had written John and Jim a letter in which he confessed a conundrum he was having with books.

> *I seem hooked on accumulating books. I was inspired to do so when, at an early age, I saw the shelves of books in the pastor's study in The Grove. I was impressed, for at home, Bibles and prayer books were the sum of what we had…. In general, I have tried to accumulate books that might have some continuing value in terms of capturing points of view, philosophies, etc., of transcending issues, as well as some biographies, novels, etc., of continuing 'life' as well…*
>
> *The essence of this note is to express the wish that the books have a 'continuing life' of their own….*

After his death, John and Jim stepped into Walter's office at the Capistrano Beach condo and looked over the walls of books — hundreds of leather-bound classics interspersed between dozens of colorful biographies, Bibles, books of quotes and poetry, and a couple dozen small paperbacks — a *bona fide* library.

Jim grabbed a book off the shelf and began to open it. The pages cracked as he pulled them apart. He set it down and opened a second book. Same thing. He scanned the shelf again, but slower this time. Nearly all the books looked as crisp as the day his father slipped them on the shelf. Jim thought it was a fitting epitaph: he'd been so busy living, he never found time to read for leisure. He also felt bad his parents never fulfilled one of their retirement goals.

That afternoon Jim said to Speedy, "I'm sorry you and dad never got to read all those books he was saving."

"Don't feel too bad," Speedy replied. "He never had time to read them; I always thought the books were just taking up space."

***

Over the next few days, John and Jim finished cleaning the condo and transferring their mom's things. As they stacked clothes and dishes, and packed boxes around the house, they discovered bottle after bottle of wine. There were entire cases stacked in obvious places like the corners of the garage and in kitchen cabinets. There were also cases and bottles tucked behind their dad's work bench, in a storage shed, stuffed in the attic space, and buried in the backs and tops of every closet throughout the house. The majority of the wine had gone bad after sitting in unventilated locations for years. The brothers took turns pouring one bad bottle after another down the sink.

When the last bottle had been emptied, John and Jim approximated how much had been poured out. By modest estimate, they accounted for at least $250,000 of fine wine, including several bottles worth upwards of $1,000. It was an ironic twist for a man who made his living cutting waste. It was also a fitting tribute.

While each bottle sat unopened and spoiling, Walter was busy pouring himself out into the world, one business, one relationship at a time. He never did get to drink that fine wine he'd been saving. Instead, others had the honor of drinking from the well of his wisdom, tenacity, and generosity. The value of the spoiled wine was nothing compared to the return his life brought. It was, in accountant speak, a wise investment.

***

Less than a week after his father's death, Jim traveled to The Grove. As he walked the main street and looked over the dilapidated buildings, weeds climbing their walls and windows long broken, he spotted the tree where his dad and Lawrence Dube once dreamed of changing the world.

He walked over and looked up at the branches. It was where it all started. He stared for a moment, taking it all in, trying to imagine his dad at eight or nine, short legs hanging off the thick branch, spouting off the latest money-making venture or the next home brewing attempt.

Jim looked down the dusty main street and tried to imagine what life had been like for his dad when his parents were gone, and it was just him, his older brothers, and the people of the town remaining. Jim wondered if the ghosts of that town knew what had become of the small boy whose life they had saved…the poor boy who never knew his dad and whose mother vanished when he was still nursing…the budding, if not mischievous, entrepreneur who was always interested in a penny and a bright future. Jim wondered if they had any idea of all his dad had accomplished in his lifetime, and all that his work had come to mean. Did they know he'd never forgotten them?

A breeze arose and blew down the dirt road and off the tumbledown brick facades. It carried the reflections Walter penned during his final year with Ernst:

When I was a boy I dreamed a lot of dreams, but I didn't dream of:
- *Owning more than one suit of clothes*
- *Traveling all over the world*
- *Living in California*
- *And personally knowing a president*

But I still get a thrill, as I did then, of:
- *A starry Texas sky*
- *A country road*
- *Bluebonnets*
- *And a small town parade*

When I was a little boy of six or seven, all my dreams seemed to have hope in them for a better world. I still have that hope. But now I know that making dreams come true is the responsibility of grown men and women.

There is no escaping the fact that the essence of an individual is his ethics. The more he seeks an ethical path, the more he mirrors the genius of his Creator – the potential of his humanity- of one who is fearfully and wonderfully made...Unless a man believes that there is a reality beyond himself to whom he owes the ultimate responsibility, his life will be fraught with ethical compromises...Our compassion must become less institutional and more personal.

Walter F. Beran